THE GOOD CALORIE DIET

THE GOOD CALORIE DIET

The Revolutionary New
Fat-Reducing
Diet Plan

PHILIP LIPETZ, PH.D

Thorsons
An Imprint of HarperCollins*Publishers*

Thorsons
An Imprint of HarperCollins*Publishers*
77–85 Fulham Palace Road,
Hammersmith, London W6 8JB

First published in the USA by HarperCollins*Publishers* Inc.,
10 East 53rd Street, New York, NY 10022, 1994
Thorsons edition 1995

1   3   5   7   9   10   8   6   4   2

© Philip Lipetz 1995

Philip Lipetz asserts the moral right
to be identified as the author of this work

A catalogue record for this book is available
from the British Library

ISBN 0 7225 3007 2

Typeset by Harper Phototypesetters Limited
Northampton, England
Printed in Great Britain by
HarperCollins Manufacturing Glasgow

Contents

Acknowledgements

I would like to thank the teachers who made this book possible: Ellis D. Lutz, high school literature; Mr Calvin, high school chemistry; Nolan Miller, college creative writing; and Ronald Hart and Karl Kornacker, graduate studies in science. All too often we ignore these people who shape our lives.

My daughter, Rebekah Devi Lipetz, helped compile the lists of Good and Bad Calories. She said that it would be one of the thrills of her young life if she could see her name in print. I just wish I had a quarter of her writing talent.

Dorothea Lipetz, my mother, helped with the daily menus. There is something pleasing about involving three generations of a family in a single project.

Larry Ashmead and Charlotte Abbott at HarperCollins furnished invaluable help in shaping this project. They missed many dinners so this book could move forward on an accelerated schedule. It was the enthusiasm they shared with Lynn Franklin, my super agent, that made it all possible. I also would like to thank Adrienne Bosworth and Sheela Tarbi for their editorial assistance, Barbara Miller for her library research assistance and generalized support, and Linda Jardine for the recipes.

Everyone who helped is a great teacher. Thank you all.

Part 1

1

Good Calories
Lower Fat Formation

MY PROMISE TO YOU

If there is one thing that the world has in abundance, it is diet plans. The Good Calorie Diet is *not* a diet plan. It is a programme that allows you to reshape your body while enjoying full meals; pounds disappear once you're on it because you stop making the new fat it takes to maintain your weight. Therefore, you can eat fully and still lose weight. Isn't such a programme better than a restrictive diet that starves or exercises you into submission?

To understand how the Good Calorie Diet works, you have to recognize that our bodies constantly make new fat and constantly burn old fat. *The balance between these two processes determines our weight.*

Thus, there are two ways to lose weight: burn more fat or make less fat. Of these two approaches, lowering the level of fat created produces much better results. Overweight people may burn 30 or 40 per cent less fat than many thin people, but, in extreme cases, they may also *create* three or four times more fat from the same quantity of certain foods. So why do conventional diets attack the lesser problem?

The Good Calorie Diet works by overcoming the metabolic condition called the Starvation Response, which stimulates the creation of fat. Even though you may eat only 1,000 calories a day, the Starvation Response makes you create the same fat as a 'thin' person does after eating 3,000 or 4,000 calories. Thus the problem is not that you eat too much, but that you *make too much fat from what you do eat.*

Once you subdue the Starvation Response and fat-creation returns to normal, weight loss occurs painlessly, without hunger or excessive exercise. Normal quantities of food will produce the low level of fat formation you may have previously achieved only with starvation diets. Without the burden of excessive fat formation, 'resting' levels of fat burning are enough to stimulate weight loss. Caloric restriction and excessive exercise are no longer needed. Your body will behave as though you were eating less even though you consume normal portions. The only thing that changes is that you make less fat.

Many modern foods and food combinations can evoke the Starvation Response in those people who are genetically susceptible to it. Fortunately, there are also some foods that inhibit the fat-creation and thereby overcome the Starvation Response. I call these miracle foods 'Good Calories'. The Good Calorie Diet is as simple as eating Good Calories and avoiding the 'Bad Calorie' foods and food combinations that create excess fat.

The weight-loss portion of the Good Calorie Diet offers so few restrictions that some people have trouble believing that something so painless can be so powerful. We all feel pretty awful on conventional diets. They make us irritable, grumpy and hungry. The reason for such discomfort is that those diets make the Starvation Response grow strong enough to alter our brain biochemistry, producing the food cravings that can trigger eating binges.

In contrast, you feel good on the Good Calorie Diet because your brain biochemistry returns to normal, and you will no longer be irritable because of hunger or cravings. You eat less because you have less of an appetite.

Conventional diets do nothing to overcome the Starvation Response. Even after you lose weight, you still form excess fat, so the moment you resume your normal eating patterns, you regain every pound of lost weight. *More than 95 per cent of dieters regain every pound.*

The dieters of the world should rise up in anger against ineffective diets that ignore the Starvation Response. Instead, dieters blame themselves. They say that their metabolisms burn less fat and that they are the exceptions to the rules of calorie counting. These dieters, and their metabolisms, are *not* exceptions to the rules. Instead, they form the overwhelming majority that proves a new rule: *the problem is* not *that you burn too little fat, but that you* make *too much fat.* You cannot permanently lose weight until you deal with this reality.

So, after the Starvation Response subsides, how fast will you lose weight? I lost over two pounds a week. Some of my friends lost less than a pound during some weeks. Still others lost four or five pounds during a week. The more overweight you are, the more quickly you will lose weight on the Good Calorie Diet. Losing twenty or thirty pounds can be simple.

I promise.

CONVENTIONAL DIETS FAIL ME

As long as you follow conventional diet programmes, it is not your fault that you remain overweight. I know because I was fat, and it was not because I was lazy. I counted calories until I had a constant ache in my belly – and my head. I joined the Columbus World Gym and pumped iron three days a week.

Even though I worked hard, it was a flabby body that sweated with effort. Whenever I looked at my jelly belly, I felt the horrible disappointment that comes from dieting without success. I even tried liposuction. Nothing worked.

If anyone should have known how to lose weight, it should have been me. I had been an assistant professor at The Ohio State University School of Medicine. I had co-authored several scientific books and dozens of articles and certainly had a sound medical background. The national press had spotlighted my work as a biotechnologist and entrepreneur. Yet I could still not lose weight.

Even though I carried only forty extra pounds, fellow scientists would comment on my weight and offer helpful suggestions. Although they meant well, this barrage of constant advice simply made me feel fatter and more inadequate.

Just as a drowning person grabs at anything that floats, I leaped at every possible clue to achieving weight loss. When anyone I knew went on a diet, I closely followed his or her progress, or lack of it.

Many championship bodybuilders – people who seemed to have perfect bodies – went to my gym. I wondered if they had the answer to my problem. After all, championship bodybuilders have less than

10 per cent body fat, compared to the typical American man with over 30 per cent body fat.

Since bodybuilders carefully note the caloric content of every morsel that passes between their lips, they seemed to be the perfect group to study, since they would quickly note the effect of any change in diet. I expected to watch them and find a simple solution, though that was not to be.

It turned out that there was no relationship between caloric intake and the amount of weight they lost. Some bodybuilders ate only 600 calories a day and could not lose the last bit of fat. Other body builders ate 3,000 to 4,000 calories a day and had bodies without an ounce of extra fat. All these people exercised for four to six hours per day. All were in good health. What accounted for the difference in their loss of fat?

CARBOHYDRATES VARY IN FAT-FORMING ABILITY

When I analysed what these bodybuilders ate, it became apparent that carbohydrates were responsible for the greatest disparities: some carbohydrates allow weight loss and others create fat. I had trouble accepting this observation, since I, too, was raised on the myth that weight loss is automatic as long as you eat fewer calories than you burn and that all calories are equal.

It took a while before I realized the flaw in this reasoning. A calorie measures the heat released when food is 'digested' in test tubes, not in people. The originators of the caloric theory of dieting assumed that our bodies use every bit of excess calories to make fat. However, scientists now know that different foods convert different percentages of calories into fat. Even though the limitations of calorie counting became obvious, nobody paid attention. The calorie theory was already the basis of a growing industry, one that ignored the Starvation Response and the realities of Good and Bad Calories.

Clearly, I had seen things that contradicted conventional diet theory. My bookshelves contained dozens of diet books, but none of these books could tell me why there was such a difference in the fat-forming potential of different carbohydrates.

From my days as a medical researcher, I knew that carbohydrates become blood sugar as they enter the bloodstream. In overweight people – and only in them – excess blood sugar becomes fat. This means that a food that creates a lot of blood sugar will produce more fat in overweight people than it will in thin people.

Conventional diets say nothing about this fact. One of the central tenets of calorie counting is that one calorie of one food creates the same amount of fat as does one calorie of another food. I saw something different. I saw that the fat-forming ability of carbohydrates can vary even when they have the same caloric content.

Excited by this new understanding, I returned to The Ohio State University Medical School and used the school's computers to search over a million scientific articles. The data I found amazed me and taught me the diet lesson of my life: the best way for overweight people to lose weight is to inhibit the formation of fat by eating the proper foods.

Hallelujah!

THE GLYCAEMIC INDEX

So how do you figure out what foods are Good Calories and create less fat? Obviously, you have to know how much blood sugar is created by each food.

Physicians use the word *glycaemic* whenever they talk about anything to do with blood sugar. When people have too much blood sugar, they are hyperglycaemic. When they have too little blood sugar, they are hypoglycaemic. When physicians measure the amount of blood sugar a food induces, they use the glycaemic index.

A high number on the glycaemic index means that a food creates more blood sugar, whereas a low number means that it causes only a small rise in blood sugar. A food with a glycaemic index of 96 (such as bananas) will create almost twice the blood sugar as a food with a glycaemic index of 50 (say, protein-enriched spaghetti). Hence, eating two portions of spaghetti creates the same amount of blood sugar as eating one portion of bananas. Therefore, eating low glycaemic-index foods allows us to eat fully while maintaining a low level of fat formation.

Hundreds of scientific reports support the notion that eating low glycaemic-index foods results in weight loss. Almost none of these reports is on weight loss, but they all are still relevant. Nearly every report indicates that altering the glycaemic index of foods changes some part of the fat-forming metabolism.

Scientists have published the glycaemic indexes of fewer than 200 foods (see chapter 11), representing a wide spectrum of common carbohydrates. Although this may seem a small number, its impact has been revolutionary.

There can be more than a sixfold difference between high- and low glycaemic-index foods (see Figure 1-1). Why is this difference important for people who suffer from the Starvation Response? High glycaemic-index foods plunge you deeper into the Starvation Response and thus make you grow fatter and make it impossible for you to lose weight permanently.

One look at Figure 1-1 told me why I was fat. I had been dieting with two meals of low-calorie rice cakes, baked potatoes, unbuttered bread, followed by a low-fat dinner. I would have lost more weight with meals of common sugar. The rice cakes created twice the blood sugar, calorie for calorie, as sugar, and the unbuttered potato created one-third more blood sugar. I could have eaten 3,000 calories of lentils, plums, grapes, or soya beans and made less fat than I would have if I'd eaten 1,000 calories of French bread and rice cakes.

I found it difficult to believe these results, yet I saw them in study after study. Foods with both a low glycaemic index and a low-to-moderate fat content represent the pot of gold at the end of the rainbow. With these foods, we can eat thousands of calories and still lose weight, by making less fat.

GOOD CALORIES AND BAD CALORIES

I gave the name Good Calories to these miracle foods that create less fat. Not surprisingly, I called foods that are high in fat-forming ability Bad Calories.

Forget about the caloric value of the food; all you have to know is whether a food is composed of Good or Bad Calories. You lose weight with Good Calories and gain weight with Bad Calories.

FIGURE 1-1

Glycaemic Index of Common Foods
(Smaller is Better)

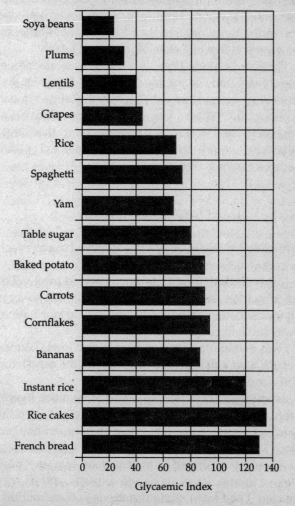

In the next few chapters you will see that Good Calories are not only beneficial diet foods, but they also defeat the Starvation Response. Thus, one simple principle is the foundation of the Good Calorie Diet: eat Good Calories until you safely overcome the Starvation Response and then lose weight effortlessly because you live in a state of improved health.

The Good Calorie Diet allows you to eat an endless variety of Good Calorie foods, while recognizing that it is only human nature to enjoy forbidden foods occasionally. After you thwart the Starvation Response, Bad Calories create less fat than they otherwise would, so you can eat them every day without creating excess fat.

IT WORKED FOR ME

With Good Calories as my foundation, I ate as much as I wanted to and still lost weight.

Just by eating Good Calories, I lowered my level of fat formation. At every meal I would push away a plate still loaded with food. It was easy to stop eating. I was full and could not eat any more.

I was no fanatic. I learned how to eat Good Calories in such a way that I could safely enjoy the occasional junk-food treat.

Even though my clothes seemed to be much looser, I refused to believe that I was losing weight. As a fat person, I associated weight loss with pain and hunger. Since I felt neither, I never weighed myself.

When my girlfriend commented on my sexy new look, I immediately weighed myself, and I was amazed. I had lost 1 stone 11 pounds in three months.

2

The Starvation Response
Creates Excess Fat

DO YOU SUFFER FROM THE
STARVATION RESPONSE?

Obviously, you suffer from the Starvation Response if
you gain weight easily and regain it even more easily
after dieting. There are several other specific
symptoms; all of them stem from the way the
Starvation Response alters your brain biochemistry so
that you eat too many of the wrong foods and then
make too much fat from them. Not all sufferers show
the same symptoms; for example, I experienced only
three or four of these symptoms.

SYMPTOMS OF THE STARVATION RESPONSE

1. Regular overeating.
2. Eating rapidly.
3. Difficulty knowing when one's stomach is full.
4. Strong or persistent hunger.
5. Craving high-fat or high-sugar food.
6. Occasional binge eating.
7. Snacking at night.
8. Gaining weight on less food.
9. Regaining weight easily.
10. Gaining weight after a pregnancy or while taking
    birth control or oestrogen-replacement pills.

1. The Starvation Response makes us overeat regularly. Ravenous hunger guarantees that our bodies will stockpile enough blood sugar to create excess fat.

2. The Starvation Response makes us eat rapidly. We have all seen hungry people wolf down a meal. That's the Starvation Response at work. Even though our minds know that our refrigerator is full of food and the grocery store is open all night, our bodies act as though this may be our last meal. It takes a while – generally about twenty minutes – before our brains realize that our stomachs are full. By eating rapidly, we consume extra food before we lose our ravenous hunger.

3. The Starvation Response prevents us from knowing when our stomachs are full. Two different hormones signal when our stomachs are full. However, the Starvation Response makes our brain ignore one of the hormones while it prevents the other from being released. The result is predictable. We don't feel full, so there is no way that we can stop eating before we overeat.

4. The Starvation Response makes us experience strong hunger. Ordinarily, a neurotransmitter in our brain controls hunger. For sufferers of the Starvation Response, that vital chemical begins to disappear. The result is an appetite that leads to obesity.

5. The Starvation Response makes us crave fattening foods. Next to obesity, the symptom most commonly shared by victims of the Starvation Response is a craving for fat and sugar: ice cream, crisps, biscuits and fizzy drinks. The problem is that the same neurotransmitter that controls our appetite also determines our cravings. If we make less of that neurotransmitter, there is no escape from the craving for fattening foods because our brain automatically enters into a programme that makes fattening foods taste good.

6. The Starvation Response makes us go on eating binges. Once our brain loses control of our eating habits, there is nothing to stop us from over-indulging. We eat more of the wrong foods without being aware that we are eating to excess.

7. The Starvation Response makes us eat late at night, when our bodies create extra fat. Late-night hunger is a sure sign that blood sugar is out of control. The Starvation Response can cause blood-sugar levels to be so low at night that there is nothing to feed our bodies. The only thing we can do is to eat an additional meal..

8. The Starvation Response makes us create more fat from what we do eat. The Starvation Response changes our body's biochemistry, so even if we eat only a small amount of food, we create more fat than would a normal person who was eating larger portions of food.

9. The Starvation Response makes us regain weight after dieting. Ordinarily, we burn or excrete excess fat rather than store it in fat cells. Now, fat moves directly into fat cells.

10. The hormonal flows within women make it harder for them to lose weight. Everyone knows that it is easier for women to gain weight and harder for them to lose it. A woman's natural hormones can unleash the Starvation Response, creating these problems after pregnancy or after taking medications that contain oestrogen.

THE GENETIC PROGRAMME
THAT CREATES FAT

To understand why we carry the genetic programme that readily creates excess fat, we have to go back in time to when our ancestors first evolved the Starvation Response.

Once, humans were rarely fat. Before the rise of the Starvation Response, the people who evolved to become modern humans lived in peace with their bodies. They ate what they found: roots, berries and vegetables. The earth was abundant. It was the world humans evolved to enjoy.

Our ancestors didn't worry about dieting or counting calories. They digested food into blood sugar and used it for short-term energy. Since food was plentiful, their bodies had more blood sugar than was needed, so they evolved hormones to keep their blood sugar low.

Then great sheets of ice descended from the polar regions of the planet. The plants that fed our ancestors vanished, along with easy days of eating food as they gathered it. The only way to eat was to hunt, and it could be days or weeks between kills. As a result, our ancestors evolved ways to maximize the conversion of excess blood sugar into stored energy in the form of body fat. Camels can live for months by digesting the fat stored in their humps. Hibernating bears live off fat during the winter sleep. Our fat can feed us for weeks and weeks. In the ice ages, it saved our ancestors' lives. Whenever they starved, they lived off stored fat.

Today our bodies still behave this way. When food intake is low, everything takes second place to the creation of fat from excess blood sugar. Having enough energy to live until the next meal is all that matters.

These ancient patterns cause the yo-yo cycle of dieting. We temporarily lose weight while we starve ourselves, but the moment we return to normal eating we become fatter than we were before we started to diet. The reason we create extra fat is simple: caloric restriction resembles starvation and evokes the Starvation Response.

This is a radically new viewpoint about the origin of obesity. The conventional explanation is that obesity is a direct result of overeating. I believe that obesity has more in common with something completely opposite – starvation.

My theory makes sense if you consider one question: when does the body most need to store excess food energy for later use – when one is eating too much food or when one faces starvation?

FATTENING FOODS AND STARVATION HAVE THE SAME EFFECT

Jack was a recent immigrant from Russia. Under the Communist regime, he was a dissident and lived under house arrest. He ate only what neighbours brought him. When he arrived in the United States, he was two or three stone underweight. However, within a year, he had gained so much weight that he was two stone overweight. He asked me to help him lose weight.

I analysed his food intake and found that he was eating about 2,000 calories per day, three-quarters of

which were from beef. He said that such meat was
unknown in Russia, so he wanted to enjoy as much of
it now as he could. Although 2,000 calories a day is
not a weight-loss diet, it certainly could not account
for the amount of weight he gained. Somehow his
previous experience with prolonged starvation had
altered his body, so he made abnormal amounts of fat
from a relatively normal diet.

I asked Jack what sort of food he ate when he was
in Russia. When he said that he ate potatoes, beetroot,
cabbage, rye bread, beans and very little meat, I was
intrigued because his new way of eating was a classic
case of evoking the Starvation Response by experiencing the excess of the modern diet. So I suggested
that he return to his old diet of carbohydrates, but not
at the old starvation levels. Instead, he should
continue to eat 2,000 calories a day.

He lost weight on the carbohydrate diet, which
proved that the caloric content of his food was
irrelevant. It was clear that his previous starvation
had changed his response to foods, but how? Why did
he continue to make excess fat and gain weight with
meat but not with carbohydrates?

The answer to these questions was first discovered in
1927, by Dr J. Shirley Sweeney, who fed different diets
to healthy medical students (see Figure 2-1 in Appendix
1).[1] One diet was high in saturated fats, one was high in
protein, and one was high in carbohydrates. The caloric
content of all three diets was the same. Another group
of students starved themselves. Each student followed
a special diet for two days and then drank a glass of
glucose. Doctors then compared the students' blood-
sugar levels to see if the students' previous means, or a
starvation diet, changed their reaction.

Sweeney found that two days of starvation induces four times more blood sugar in a future meal than does a carbohydrate diet, a fatty diet creates almost as much blood sugar, and a protein diet causes a threefold increase. Later studies confirmed Sweeney's discovery.[2]

Sweeney's results explain why many people are overweight even though they may not experience starvation. Many meals we eat are high in protein and fat and mimic the long-term consequences of starvation by pushing the body to create extra fat from all subsequent meals.

Why do fat and protein induce the same response as starvation? To answer this question, we have to go back to the time when our ancestors switched from food gathering to hunting.

Our ancestors ate meat and fat only when starvation forced them to deviate from their normal vegetable- and fruit-eating patterns. It was simply too difficult to hunt with the primitive weapons available in those times, and there were days or weeks between kills. Our ancestors' bodies adapted to conditions during which days or weeks of hunger always followed meals of meat and fat. Deep within our DNA is the genetic memory of these times. In some people, this memory still actively drives their behaviour. Even today, the bodies of susceptible people respond to meat, fat and high blood sugar by gearing up for the starvation that may follow, by making more fat.

This starvation response is also why caloric-restriction diets fail. After restricting the number of calories they consume, dieters resume eating normally, but they are doomed. Even eating a reasonable number of calories, 1,500 per day, is fattening if the 1,500 calories create the same amount of blood sugar that a thin person would create with 6,000 calories. Who would not gain weight on 6,000 calories a day?

CREATING FAT FROM EXCESS BLOOD SUGAR

When I was in college, I dated a woman whom I shall call Laura. Laura was full of fire, eager to explore the new horizons open to women. She also had a chocolate addiction and ate nearly half a pound per day. However, the chocolate never affected her weight. Laura was a slim beauty.

After graduation, we went our separate ways. It was nearly a year before I saw her again. She had developed high blood sugar and was returning home for treatment. We both knew that her constant consumption of chocolate was probably the cause. What I did not expect to find was that Laura had gained two stone. When she lost control of her blood sugar, her fat forming metabolism changed, so that her excessive caloric intake now mattered.

Laura was my first great love, and I have always remembered her. Over the years, as I pursued a scientific career, I wondered why her excess blood sugar turned into fat.

Ordinarily, excess blood sugar does not contribute to the formation of fat.[3] Lean people burn excess blood sugar or store it as glycogen, a sugar-water complex. The bodies of lean people convert blood sugar into fat only when their glycogen stores are saturated.[4]

When we experience the Starvation Response, we

lose the ability to store or burn excess blood sugar.[5] Blood sugar cannot be stored as glycogen because the enzyme needed to convert blood sugar into glycogen is 50 per cent to 85 per cent less active.[6] Furthermore, we create so much more blood sugar that we would exceed the capacity of our glycogen stores even if that pathway was fully active.

The resulting excess blood sugar becomes fat.[7] People who suffer from the Starvation Response convert up to three to four times *more* blood sugar to triglyceride fats (the fats that pass into fat cells), creating more permanent body weight than thin people.[8]

In 1988 a group of Swiss researchers deliberately induced the Starvation Response in their subjects with a four-day high-fat diet and then induced excess blood sugar by feeding the subjects a high carbohydrate diet.[9] Their experiment (see Figure 2-2 in Appendix 1) shows that people who experience the Starvation Response have a vastly increased capacity to convert excess blood sugar into fat. After the high carbohydrate diet, the subjects exhibited more than a tenfold increase in triglyceride fats.

This is why you must avoid the Starvation Response: it makes you create more fat from carbohydrates, as happened to Laura. When Laura began to suffer from the Starvation Response, excessive consumption of chocolate caused her body to create more fat.

PUTTING FAT INTO FAT CELLS

Ann lost over two stone using conventional caloric

restriction. Then she ate a meagre amount of food and exercised constantly to maintain her weight loss. Despite all this effort, she found that the only way she could keep her ideal weight was by eating a diet that was extremely low in fat.

I told Ann that her dieting had altered her body, so that any fat in her bloodstream was moved directly into permanent fat stores. I suggested that she go to the Good Calorie Diet, not to lose weight but to overcome the Starvation Response. When she did, both her cravings and her intolerance of fat disappeared. An unexpected bonus was that she found she could eat more food and exercise less without gaining weight.

Creating excess fats from carbohydrates is only part of the process of obesity. Enzymes, including lipoprotein lipase, must also ease the movement of fat into fat cells.[10] People who experience the Starvation Response have supercharged levels of lipoprotein lipase activity – up to 30 times more than a normal person would experience (see Figure 2-3 in Appendix 1),[11] and their lipoprotein lipase activity remains high until they regain just a little more weight than they lost.[12]

Any diet that ignores the Starvation Response must be extremely low in dietary fat to compensate for excess fat formation. Since the Good Calorie Diet thwarts this problem, you do not have to confine yourself to such a rigorous regime. Moderate fat is fine.

MAKING US EAT MORE

While I was writing this book, a friend of mine approached me. Although she is a successful musician and directs a famous music festival, she felt inadequate because she was overweight and could not lose the extra pounds. Her physicians and friends all said that she lacked willpower, but that was not my impression of this wonderful woman. No one could have been as successful as she without discipline.

I told her that she was a victim of the Starvation Response and explained that her body was selectively ignoring insulin's normal ability to lower blood sugar and decrease appetite, though it did not ignore insulin's activation of fat-forming enzymes. This state, known as *insulin resistance*, is almost universally accepted as a characteristic of obese people.[13]

Triggered by the *same things* that evoke the Starvation Response,[14] insulin resistance interferes with three of the systems that control eating. Ordinarily, eating produces an insulin rush that enters the nervous system and limits our appetite. Insulin resistance makes us ignore this signal.[15] Instead, high levels of insulin make fats and sweets seem more desirable.[16] Second, insulin resistance inhibits the release of glucagon, the hormone that signals when our stomachs are full.[17] Finally, insulin resistance suppresses serotonin, a neurotransmitter that prevents the craving of carbohydrates and excessive appetites.[18]

As I told my friend, you can stop feeling guilty about your inability to control your appetite. You are a good person with sufficient willpower. You eat the wrong foods, and more of them, because you suffer from the Starvation Response.

THE STARVATION RESPONSE AND WOMEN

Since the nutrients that enter a woman's body can be diverted to support her foetus or nursing child, women have evolved the equivalent of periods of starvation that can induce the Starvation Response. Women carry this programme even if they are not pregnant.

The signal that induces this type of Starvation Response appears to be related to oestrogen, a sex hormone. When extra levels of oestrogen are present, a woman's fat cells become enlarged. It is the oestrogen released during adolescence that causes women to accumulate fat on their hips and thighs.

When women take birth control pills or oestrogen-replacement pills for menopause, they may trigger the Starvation Response. If they cannot lose weight, then they should consult a doctor about the possibility of lowering their dosage of oestrogen.

For women, consuming animal fats can be extra fat-forming because these Bad Calories increase the production of oestrogen.[19]

Despite these problems, women need not assume that they cannot lose weight just because they are female. No matter what the inducing factor, the Good Calorie Diet treats the ultimate problem – the Starvation Response.

THE STARVATION RESPONSE IS A COLLECTION OF MANY DIFFERENT CONDITIONS

I will conclude this chapter by emphasizing that the Starvation Response is made up of a wide variety of metabolic variations that all cause the formation of excessive fat. These differences arose because each racial group evolved its own solution to the problem of creating excess fat. Any of the following can result in the increased formation of fat:

1. high blood sugar
2. high insulin levels
3. high triglyceride levels
4. high lipid levels
5. high lipoprotein lipase levels
6. impaired fat burning
7. insulin resistance
8. decreased excretion of fat
9. variations in female hormones
10. other enzyme functions

Clearly, this is an open-ended description of a wide variety of clinical symptoms. That is why the Good Calorie Diet includes a programme of controlled experimentation that allows you to tailor a programme for yourself that overcomes your version of the Starvation Response. Such a programme guarantees that each person will enjoy the maximum freedom to choose certain foods and to achieve the maximum results.

I should mention that thin people can also suffer from the Starvation Response, remaining thin until the wrong diet exposes them to high amounts of fat or protein or the restriction of calories.[20] Thus, the Starvation Response can be a hidden time bomb, waiting for the wrong diet to detonate it.

That was my experience. I had always thought of myself as a person who could eat without worrying about gaining weight. I always ate second and third helpings and yet maintained an average weight of 12¹/₂ stone. Then I got divorced and wanted to look more attractive as I began to develop a new social life. When I was about to go snorkeling in Florida, I went on a high protein-low carbohydrate diet and lost five or six pounds. Within the next two months, I gained a stone. Within a year, I had ballooned to nearly 15¹/₂ stone. Clearly, my diet had unleashed the Starvation Response.

3

Avoiding the Problems
of the Modern Diet

MODERN FOODS EVOKE THE STARVATION RESPONSE

Think of the irony. We live in a land of plenty and eat foods whose richness and sweetness would have dazzled ancient kings. Yet, in the midst of all this abundance, our bodies can behave as though we face starvation.

The problem is simple. We eat an abundance of high-energy foods that resemble the foods our ancestors ate when starvation forced them to hunt. Following genetically programmed patterns of survival, our bodies interpret this diet to mean that we face starvation. So our bodies make extra blood sugar and convert that food energy into fat.

Not only do we eat more Bad Calories now, but the modern diet is low in the Good Calories that can prevent the Starvation Response. In 1860 Good Calories accounted for over half the food we ate (see Figure 3-1 in Appendix 1). In the 1920s they made up just under 40 per cent of our diet. Twenty years ago, they constituted no more than one quarter of our diet. Who knows what today's figure is?

If we understand what elements of the modern diet evoke or perpetuate the Starvation Response, we can then take the first step toward curing it. Just by avoiding a few foods and food combinations, we can decrease our formation of fat. We will still eat fully. There will be no difference in our caloric intake.

Foods that induce the Starvation Response all have one thing in common: none was part of our ancestors' normal diet. So why are we surprised that our bodies panic when they are exposed to foods that signal the absence of 'normal foods'?

This understanding means that we must adopt a new mind-set when we use the Good Calorie Diet. A conventional diet allows us to eat any low-fat food, but in lesser amounts than we otherwise might. The Good Calorie Diet says we are better off choosing the proper foods and then eating as much of them as we want.

So which is more restrictive: starving on an infinite variety of foods or eating as much as we want of the proper foods? I prefer that my stomach is full and that my body is disease free. My mind no longer misses unhealthy foods or combinations of foods; instead it looks on them as a form of poison that I have finally learned to avoid. How can I miss eating something that made me grow fat?

AN EASY WAY TO LOSE WEIGHT

'I'm a good friend of yours, why won't you give me a copy of your book?'

I heard this request constantly while writing this book, and it always presented me with a dilemma. Should I give out only a portion of the entire book or make my friends wait for the entire manuscript? One friend, Marianne, was $1^1/2$ stone overweight and was going on a vacation, where she intended to meet the man of her dreams. She didn't care that I had written only a few chapters. She believed she could make herself more attractive if only I would give them to her. I gave in, not because I think that the Good Calorie Diet can be split into small pieces, but because I wanted to boost Marianne's self-confidence. I gave her this chapter.

To my complete amazement, Marianne lost ten pounds in a month. She did less than the complete programme and thus never lost the last ten pounds, but Marianne did not care. She was slimmer and felt more beautiful.

It thrilled me that the tricks contained in this chapter were so powerful. I know that without the benefit of my full Good Calorie programme, these tricks are not enough to overcome the Starvation Response. So Marianne still stands a good chance of regaining all the weight she lost. Furthermore, she did not lose all the weight that she wanted to lose and would have lost had she used the entire programme.

You will apply these tricks throughout the entire Good Calorie Diet. Remember that the foods that evoke the Starvation Response must be considered a special class of Bad Calories and that one of the cornerstones of the programme is to avoid Bad Calories.

This rule brings up the question of practicality. Bad Calories may be difficult to avoid altogether in the modern diet. Must you be fanatical about avoiding them? Obviously, to do so would be inconvenient. Therefore, the Good Calorie Diet is a two-stage programme. While the first stage tames the Starvation

Response, you should be vigilant about observing the suggestions of the programme. After you stop making excess fat, you will enter a period when you can experiment to see if your genetics will allow you to violate some of these rules occasionally.

Eventually you will find your limits. You will know how many Bad Calories you can tolerate without provoking the formation of excess fat. Then you can stay thin by merely staying within those limits.

The Good Calorie Diet could have been designed arbitrarily to eliminate all Bad Calories. However, because the Starvation Response is a collection of different genetic programmes, there is no need to avoid food and combinations of foods that are harmful only to someone else.

Now we will consider the tricks that eliminate adverse physiological signals of the modern diet. They do not constitute the entire Good Calorie Diet, but only those problems that induce the Starvation Response.

In brief, this is the list of tricks:

AVOID THINGS THAT INCREASE FAT FORMATION

Avoid foods that are high in fat.
Avoid saturated fats; substitute unsaturated fats.
Avoid overcooked carbohydrates.
Avoid overly ripe fruit.
Avoid processed foods.
Avoid canned starches and legumes.
Avoid fructos.
Avoid alcohol before a meal.
Avoid smoking before a meal.
Avoid Bad Calories before and during exercise.

Avoid foods that are high in fat. Over the past 100 years, the percentage of calories that the average person derives from fat has increased (see Table 3-1).[1] This is a disaster. The ingestion of large amounts of fat decreases the rate at which we burn energy, making it harder to lose weight.[2] It also ignites the Starvation Response, making it easy to manufacture more fat.[3]

TABLE 3-1

Percentage of Calories in our Diet from Three Sources

	1860	1920	1975
Protein	12	12	14
Fat	25	32	43
Carbohydrate	63	56	43

How much fat is too much? Many governmental agencies recommend that no more than 30 per cent of our daily calories should be from fat. I accept this recommendation. Therefore, any food that derives more than 30 per cent of its calories from fat is a Bad Calorie.

Why do I *not* recommend that you follow an extremely low-fat diet? Because it alters your physiology, so you will create more fat from blood sugar.[4] Your appetite will also increase.[5] What is even more important is that there is no need for an extremely low-fat diet when you substitute unsaturated fats for animal fats.

People with extremely high levels of cholesterol, atherosclerosis, or heart disease should not take this recommendation to mean that an extremely low-fat diet won't help treat their diseases. For these people, an extremely low-fat diet can be a lifesaver. I recommend that they follow the Good Calorie Diet while watching their fat intake, though they should consult with their doctor first.

Practical Suggestions: As I will explain in the next section, sometimes a low-fat food that is high on the glycaemic index can produce more fat than can a high glycaemic-index food combined with the proper amount of vegetable fat; therefore, you should not automatically consume any food that is advertised as being low in fat.

Avoid saturated fats; substitute unsaturated fats. Dietary studies that recommend a low-fat diet usually refer to the elimination of saturated animal fats. I agree that saturated fats should make up less than 10 per cent of your caloric intake. However, diets that are extraordinarily low in fat seem unnecessary when the beneficial effects of unsaturated fats are considered.

Unsaturated (vegetable) fats, but not saturated (animal) fats, inhibit the creation of fat from carbohydrates (see Figure 3-2 in Appendix 1).[6] Butter, a saturated fat, increases the glycaemic index of bread by over 20 per cent, whereas olive oil and corn oil, both unsaturated fats, reduce the glycaemic index of bread by over 70 per cent. Olive oil is better than corn oil for reducing blood sugar.[7]

Thus, eating a little unsaturated fat may actually reduce the total fat you create when you are faced with meals of Bad Calorie carbohydrates. Say that you *have* to eat garlic bread. Since there is a lot of bread and it will make a lot of fat, you will get ahead of the game by adding a *small* amount of unsaturated corn oil margarine, which lowers the amount of fat created from the bread. However, the *best* solution would be to avoid the garlic bread altogether.

Unsaturated fats also help you lose weight in three other ways. First, when you eat a high ratio of unsaturated to saturated fats, you create less fat than if all those fat calories were saturated fat.[9] Second, your body *prefers* to burn unsaturated fats, rather than to place them in fat cells.[10] Third, in people who suffer from the Starvation Response, but not in lean people, the metabolism of other foods is 50 per cent higher after meals that are high in unsaturated fats.[11] All this means that substituting unsaturated fats for saturated fats will make you lose weight even if you do not decrease your intake of calories.

There are five primary sources of saturated fats in the Western diet: dairy products, cooking oils, animal fat, processed foods and chocolates. Most vegetable fats are unsaturated. Common unsaturated vegetable oils include canola oil, corn oil, olive oil, peanut oil, safflower oil, sesame oil, soybean oil and sunflower oil. A note of caution is warranted here: not all vegetable oils are unsaturated fats. Avocados and nuts are high in saturated fats. So are the coconut, palm, and palm kernel oils that are frequently used in processed foods and sweets.

When I was developing the Good Calorie Diet, there was a question of how to use fat to lower the glycaemic index of Bad Calorie carbohydrates. Some nutritionists thought they could counter Bad Calorie breads and potatoes by combining them with butter or meats that contain fats. The problem with this solution is twofold. First, meat contains saturated fats that raise, not lower, the fat-forming potential of carbohydrates. Second, meat contains protein, which should not be combined with starches, such as bread and potatoes, because this combination raises the glycaemic index of the resulting meal (see Chapter 6).

Practical Suggestions: Chip lovers who cannot survive without chips should find a place that fries the potatoes in unsaturated vegetable oil because then the carbohydrate content of the Bad Calorie will do them less harm. However, remember that you cannot lose weight on a constant diet of chips, even those that are cooked in unsaturated fat.

You shall see that in the early part of the Good Calorie Diet, you are asked to decrease your consumption of animal products. You do so to avoid not only the protein that evokes the Starvation Response, but the saturated fats that accompany animal products.

You can enjoy the benefits of unsaturated fats only when a small percentage of your fat intake consists of saturated fats, so you should remove most saturated animal fats from your diet.[12] Almost all red meats and dairy products are high in saturated fats. Chicken and turkey also have more saturated than unsaturated fats, but they have a better ratio of unsaturated to saturated fats than red meat.

Fish often have a better ratio of unsaturated to saturated fats than red meat, but not all fish are high in unsaturated fat (see Table 3-2). You can cut your consumption of saturated fat by up to 75 per cent by switching from red meat to the proper fish. Therefore, you can improve your creation of fat simply by substituting fish for meat.

TABLE 3.2

Unsaturated Fat in Fish

Fish with More Unsaturated Fat	Fish with Less Unsaturated Fat
Bass, striped	Abalone
Clams	Catfish
Cod	Gefilte fish
Crab	Herring
Haddock	Lobster
Halibut	Mussels
Perch	Oyster
Pike, northern	Pompano
Salmon, Atlantic, coho, pink	Roughy
	Sablefish
Scallops	Salmon, chinook, chum
Shrimp	Sea trout
Sea bass	Sturgeon
Snapper	Swordfish
Trout	
Tuna	
Whitefish	
Whiting	

Although I recommend eating unsaturated fats, do not take it as a licence to consume excess fat. No one should use too much fat of any type. If you are suffering from the Starvation Response, most fat calories go directly into fat cells. However, when you do consume fat, just make sure that it is unsaturated fat.

Avoid overcooked carbohydrates. Eating overcooked foods can double the blood sugar available for conversion into fat. Why does overcooking do so?

Because it destroys the fibres needed to prevent carbohydrates from being converted into blood sugar.

You can lower a carbohydrate's fat-forming potential by slightly under-cooking it. This rule applies to almost all sources of carbohydrates – rice, potatoes and vegetables. All pastas, except canned pasta, appear to be an exception to this rule. It is one of the simplest weight-loss tricks.

Figure 3-3 in Appendix 1 shows what happens with rice. Instant rice cooked for six minutes produces double the blood sugar of instant rice cooked for one minute. Without changing the caloric content, overcooking doubles the rice's fat-forming ability.

Practical Suggestions: Some Chinese restaurants overcook rice or use glutenous rice because it helps the rice kernels stick together, so they can be easily eaten with chopsticks. The glycaemic index of glutenous rice is nearly 100, or almost double that of properly cooked rice.

If you order a potato or another starch, slightly underdone, you may halve the fat it creates.

Stews and soups tend to feature overcooked carbohydrates, so be careful when ordering these items.

Avoid overly ripe fruit. As a fruit ripens, its sugars break down into simple, and better-tasting, sugars that have higher glycaemic indexes. Therefore avoid excessively ripe fruits; they create excess fat.

Bananas are a perfect example of how the ripeness of a fruit influences its glycaemic index. Starch is the principal ingredient in an underripe banana, a low glycaemic-index carbohydrate. As the banana ripens its starch turns into free sugars, and the glycaemic index increases by 70 per cent, changing the fruit from a Good Calorie one to a Bad Calorie one.[13] Although there have been no scientific studies, the same process is likely to occur with other fruits, such as pears and peaches.

Practical Suggestions: You do not have to eat green, unripe fruit. Rather, choose firm yellow bananas and avoid mushy, brown-spotted ones. Other fruits do not have to be hard; choose soft but not mushy or obviously juicy ones.

Many health bars sell fruit drinks that are freshly prepared in a blender. Frequently, they use overly ripe fruit (so no one will see the condition of the fruit). It's probably best to avoid those that do.

Avoid processed foods. Food processing includes a wide variety of manufacturing techniques that make food easier to handle or to use. The more processed the food, the more blood sugar it makes. Dr Janet Brand and her colleagues at the University of Sydney found that processing increased the glycaemic index of corn by 60 per cent; of rice, by 90 per cent; and of potatoes, by 50 per cent (see Table 3-3).[14]

Practical Suggestions: Most ready-to-eat foods – including almost any food on a shelf in a food shop – that are packaged in a bag or a box are processed foods. Foods that have been pre-cooked or altered so they take less time to cook are processed foods. All are Bad Calories and can be eaten only in accordance with the rules in Chapter 5.

TABLE 3.3

Food Processing Increases the Glycaemic
Indexes of Foods

Food	Glycaemic Index
Potatoes	100
Instant potatoes	156
Corn	100
Corn chips	152
Cornflakes	163
Rice	100
Instant Rice	178
Puffed rice	190

Avoid canned starches and legumes. Canning drastically increases the glycaemic index of starches. Canned pasta, for example, has twice the glycaemic index of home-cooked pasta.[15] It also stimulates the body to release nearly 50 per cent more insulin, thereby activating fat-forming enzymes.

Canning also doubles the glycaemic index of legumes, such as kidney beans and lentils. Thus it raises them from the best Good Calories of foods with barely acceptable levels on the glycaemic index.

Practical Suggestions: Canned pasta lies hidden within minestrone, chicken noodle, and many other canned soups; watch out for it. Those canned soups that do not contain canned pasta usually contain beans or other legumes whose glycaemic index is raised by canning. Therefore, try to avoid canned soups; dehydrated soups are no better.

Most canned children's foods contain pasta. Even if

your children are not generally overweight, it is not a good idea to feed them foods that induce the Starvation Response. Remember, the Starvation Response is a genetically programmed response and hence the children of sufferers have a high probability of being susceptible.

Avoid fructose. The most commonly used sweetener in manufactured foods is corn syrup. Fructose, the active ingredient, is a greater part of the Western diet than sugar. The average person consumes 15 per cent of his or her calories as fructose.[16]

Of the many forms of sugar in our diet, fructose is the easiest for the body to convert into fat.[17] When it is combined with fat, such as in a chocolate bar, fructose is capable of producing more new fat than sugar.[18]

What is most remarkable about fructose sweetener is that it may be harmless for people who do not suffer from the Starvation Response, but it is fattening for those that do. Fructose sweetener increases insulin levels and insulin resistance in people who are predisposed to high levels of insulin or blood sugar (see Figure 3-4 in Appendix 1).[19] Although it has no effect on men who do not suffer from the Starvation Response, fructose sweetener increases the synthesis of triglycerides by more than 50 per cent in men who do suffer (see Figure 3-5 in Appendix 1).[20] Strangely, it does not affect female non-sufferers in the same way. I do not know of any studies showing the effect fructose sweetener has on women who experience the Starvation Response.

Practical Suggestions: It is not easy to avoid fructose

sweetener. If you are to have a normal lifestyle, you must practise moderation. What you can do is avoid products such as jams and sweets, in which fructose or corn syrup sweetener is one of the two major ingredients, listed as the first or second ingredient on the nutritional label.

Does this mean that you should avoid fresh fruits that contain high levels of natural fructose? There is no evidence to support such an action. Many studies have found that there is a difference between natural sweeteners and commercially processed sweeteners. It appears that the refining of sugars makes them less nutritionally desirable. So my advice is to eat fresh fruits and don't worry about unrefined fructose.

Avoid alcohol before a meal. Alcohol raises blood sugar just as strongly as if it were the worst Bad Calorie. If you drink alcohol before a meal, it turns the food that follows into Bad Calories by raising your blood-sugar response.[23]

Practical Suggestions: If you want an alcoholic drink, have it two or three hours before a meal or two hours after a meal. If you drink alcohol too soon before a meal, you'll create excess blood sugar that is diverted into the formation of fat. Similarly, it's best to give your body a chance to finish absorbing food before drinking anything that will change your fat-forming metabolism.

If you must have alcohol with your meal, drink it late in the meal, and then only if you are eating a meal rich in Good Calories.

Be aware, however, that some people will have a difficult time escaping from the Starvation Response if they continue to drink alcohol.

Avoid smoking before or during meals. Swedish doctors reported that aside from its other harmful effects, smoking produces a sudden rise in blood sugar, followed by a sharp decrease immediately after the nicotine high vanishes.[24] This reaction can increase the formation of fat. When you can possibly do so, you should let more than an hour pass between smoking and eating.

Some people use smoking as a dietary aid. They would rather fill their mouths with cigarettes than with food. This strategy is doomed to backfire because low blood sugar response will increase their appetite.

Avoid bad calories before and during exercise. Exercise helps you to lose weight by lowering blood-sugar levels, reversing insulin resistance and lowering triglycerides.[25] However, ingesting Bad Calorie carbohydrates before or during aerobic and anaerobic exercise makes you burn glycogen instead of blood sugar and promotes insulin resistance, thus increasing the availability of blood sugar for the formation of fat.[26] This problem is particularly relevant because most exercise drinks, including many that are designed to replace electrolytes, are Bad Calories. When you consume these drinks while exercising, you negate the benefits of exercise.

Practical Suggestions: If you exercise, eat Good Calorie meals or exercise moderately so that Bad Calories will have less of a negative impact. The U.S. Centres for Disease Control recently announced that people do not need to exercise vigorously to experience the benefits of aerobic exercise. Rather, 30 minutes of moderate exercise, four times a week, is enough.[27] The president of the American College of Sports Medicine suggested that 'people can climb stairs instead of riding elevators and escalators. They can garden. They can rake leaves, they can dance. They can walk part or all of the way to work.' 'We made a mistake by insisting that it must be sustained aerobic activity,' said the director of epidemiology at the Cooper Institute of Aerobics Research.

What about anaerobic exercises, such as those found in the slow movements of hatha yoga, tai chi, weight lifting, and isometrics? These exercises now qualify as moderate aerobic exercises, and, according to the new guidelines, are as helpful as are strenuous aerobic exercises.

One quick note for my bodybuilding friends. Anabolic steroids increase insulin and decrease the ability to regulate blood sugar.[28] Clearly, they contribute to the Starvation Response.

4

Good and Bad Calories

WHAT MAKES A FOOD INTO A GOOD CALORIE?

Good Calories represent the pot of gold at the end of the rainbow. With them, you can eat thousands of calories and still lose weight because you make less fat.

Creating a list of Good Calorie foods is more complicated than simply selecting every food with a low glycaemic index because the glycaemic index of a food can be lowered by its fat content. Thus, some low glycaemic-index foods are high in fat, and none of us wants a diet of high-fat foods. Sweets, chocolate, pâté and high-fat ice cream all have low glycaemic indexes but a high-fat content. We should not eat them. Although at least two books have proposed weight-loss diets that include high-fat foods with low glycaemic indexes, no one can lose weight on such diets. Such an idea may sell books, but it is absurd. Good Calories must derive 30 per cent or less of their calories from fat.

Where is the dividing line between Good Calories and Bad Calories? Clearly, sugar is fat inducing, so let's use it as the dividing point. Any food that derives less than 31 per cent of its calories from fat and has a glycaemic index lower than sugar is a Good Calorie, and any food with more fat or a higher glycaemic index is a Bad Calorie. Among the Good Calories are rice, spaghetti, yams, grapes, lentils, and plums.[1] Among the Bad Calories are almost all types of bread, carrots, rice cakes, processed breakfast cereals and white potatoes.

If you use the list of Good and Bad Calories in Chapter 12, you do not have to calculate the percentage of calories from fat. If you still want to calculate the percentage of calories that are derived from fat, multiply the grams of fat in a portion (9 calories in a gram of fat, and 4 calories in a gram of carbohydrate) by 9 and divide that figure by the total number of calories in the portion. For example, if one portion of a food has 140 calories and 6 grams of fat, then that portion contains 54 grams of fat (6x9=54), and 38.6 per cent of the calories are from fat (54÷140=.386). So the next time some product advertises that it contains only 6 grams of fat, you should realize that that number may still be more than the 30 per cent maximum allowed for a Good Calorie food. In fact, listing the grams of fat instead of the calories of fat is a deceptive labelling practice.

GOOD CALORIES

The following sections present an overview of the wide variety of Good Calorie foods in Chapter 12.

Rye bread. Unlike breads made from wheat flour, rye bread has a low glycaemic index. Therefore, pumpernickel and rye breads are good substitutes for modern white breads.

Be careful though. Many pumpernickel and rye breads have more wheat flour than rye and thus have a greater fat-forming potential. The easiest way to tell which flour predominates is to examine the list of ingredients. If wheat flour is listed before rye flour, it means that there is more wheat flour in the bread.

Until this century, pumpernickel formed the basis of many European diets. Perhaps this is the reason why obesity is a modern phenomenon in those countries.

Whole-grain breads. Substituting whole or cracked grains for milled flour lowers the glycaemic index of bread[2] and can turn wheat bread from a Bad Calorie into a Good Calorie. However, just the addition of kernels of whole grain does not guarantee that a wheat bread will have a low glycaemic index. The bread may have to consist of at least 50 per cent to 75 per cent whole kernels.

Many breads are marketed as whole-grain breads but are not composed of intact kernels. Rather, they contain milled flour made from the whole kernel. Althouth this type of flour increases the availability of certain nutrients, it does nothing to lower the glycaemic index of the bread.

I have included a list of acceptable breads on page 223.[3] These are breads that list whole- or sprouted-wheat grains as the first, and primary, ingredient. Although they are good enough to be listed as Good Calories, they are just barely good enough. They still have much higher glycaemic indexes than whole rye flour bread. Eat wheat bread sparingly.

There are two other ways to make wheat bread or other bakery products so they will be extremely low on the glycaemic index: by increasing the size of the wheat particles[4] or by adding viscous fibre, such as guar gum.[5] Unfortunately, I do not know any nationally distributed breads that are prepared this way. However, the coarsely ground wheat breads in India are reported to have a glycaemic index that is only one-third that of modern bread. So it is not impossible to prepare such breads commercially.

If you cannot find Good Calorie bread, you may have to make the difficult decision to give up bread. Bad Calorie breads are one of the prime contributors to the Starvation Response.

Pasta. Since it is made from wheat flour, scientists expected pasta to have a high glycaemic index, similar to bread, but it does not. Pasta is a Good Calorie.

It appears that the process of extruding dough through a cold press changes the fibres of pasta and lowers its glycaemic index. Perhaps scientists will soon learn how to apply this same technique to other wheat products. It would be a pleasure to see bread with a low glycaemic index.

When you eat pasta, it is important to avoid mixing it with large quantities of animal protein (see Chapter 6). A small amount of animal protein in the sauce is fine, but a large amount transforms the meal into a Bad Calorie disaster.

Drinks. The best drinks are decaffeinated and lack natural sweeteners. They include water, diet soda, decaffeinated coffee and tea, herbal tea, fruit juice and vegetable juice.

It is important to drink sufficient quantities of liquid in between meals rather than only with meals. Doing so avoids diluting your digestive enzymes by excessive drinking during meals.

Oatmeal. Old-fashioned slow-cooked oatmeal (cooked for six or more minutes) is the perfect breakfast food. Many Scandinavians eat breakfasts laden with fatty meats, yet they avoid obesity because they combine meats with oatmeal. Although this is not a recommended practice, it does show the power of oatmeal.

Be sure to avoid instant varieties of oatmeal. They have a much higher glycaemic index.

Chicken and turkey. After you overcome the Starvation Response, low-fat chicken or turkey is a Good Calorie food. You should avoid combining either with starch or fruit (see Chapter 6). Eat chicken or turkey during the noon meal.

All white meats, except wings, are acceptable. Skinless dark meats, except thighs, are also Good Calories. When possible, avoid the skin.

The major problem with poultry is that it has a high ratio of saturated to unsaturated fats. Therefore, you must be careful about combining poultry with starches.

Chilli. Although meat chilli is almost universally high in fat, products made with chicken or vegetarian substitutes are Good Calories.

Low-fat dairy products. Diet cheese, low-fat milk, low-fat cottage cheese, and low-fat ice cream are all Good Calories.

Some people are unable to digest lactose, the sugar in milk. For them, lactose creates digestive problems that can turn dairy products into Bad Calories. The symptoms are bloating, gas, diarrhoea and discomfort. The solution is to use reduced-lactose products or to take lactose enzyme pills.

Fish. Good Calorie fish include bass, cod, crab, flounder, haddock, halibut, lobster, perch, wild salmon, (not farm-bred) scrod, scallops, prawn, snapper and tuna canned in water.

It is best to eat fish that are high in unsaturated fats (see Chapter 3). This fish can be more safely combined with starches, but only in small quantities.

Some types of fish are high in fat and should be avoided. These include some forms of farm-bred salmon. Check the source of your salmon.

As with other protein products, consume fish after curing the Starvation Response and, when possible, at the noon meal. Avoid back-to-back fish meals.

Frozen dinners. Not all convenience food is junk. At the same time, few convenience foods are nutritionally equal to freshly prepared meals.

To determine if frozen dinners are Good Calories, judge them as a whole. A Good Calorie dinner may contain foods that would be Bad Calories if they were eaten individually. Be careful to eat the entire meal or at least an equal percentage of each food. The most common error is to eat a Bad Calorie main dish and ignore the vegetables.

Another common error is to eat a Bad Calorie dessert or entrée before you eat the Good Calories. This practice is almost as bad as eating only Bad Calories because it will flood your body with blood sugar and insulin *before* you take your first mouthful of Good Calories.

Fruit. Almost all fruits are Good Calories. However, avoid dried fruits, fruits packaged in syrup, and overly ripe fruit, since these have high glycaemic indexes.

Pizza. Pizza is made from wheat and cheese, each of which is a Bad Calorie. Taken together, wheat and cheese can form a Good Calorie because the fat in the cheese lowers the glycaemic index of the bread crust.

Just make sure that less than 30 per cent of the calories in the pizza come from fat. Generally, a pizza with slightly less than a single portion of cheese and no meat topping fulfills this requirement.

Deep-dish pizzas typically have a greater fat content than do thin-crust pizzas.

The same principle applies to cheese sandwiches.

Legumes (beans). Legumes are the lowest glycaemic-index food. Combining them with other foods is one of the most powerful principles of the Good Calorie Diet. Legumes will drastically reduce the amount of blood sugar produced by the resulting meal.

Though the Hindu diet is composed of many Bad Calories, many meals are preceded by dhal soups, composed of lentils. Lentils are so low on the glycaemic index that you can eat eight times more lentils than rice cakes and still make less fat. Eating lentils protects Indians against their genetic tendency to become obese.[6] Perhaps it is no coincidence that lentils form such an important part of the Indian diet that Indian newspapers list the prices of over 300 varieties.

It is easy for Westerners to do the same thing: start meals with bean soup and serve peas or beans with main dishes. There are many ways to prepare legumes. You should use them to accelerate your weight loss. Time and time again, I have seen people kick their diets into high gear with legumes.

You can create a perfect substitute for animal protein by combining 1 part legume with $2^1/2$ parts of grains, such as rice. This combination produces a mixture of amino acids that is optimal for creating muscle. One of the greatest bodybuilders of all time,

Bill Pearl, used legumes and grains to build and maintain his Mr Universe body on a vegetarian diet. Mexicans do the same thing when they combine beans and corn in burritos, as do Indians when they eat dhal lentils with native breads.

A note of caution: soya beans are very low on the glycaemic index, but tofu is made with fermented soya beans and should be avoided because its fat content may be as high as 70 per cent of its caloric content. Canning also increases the glycaemic index of legumes.

Mexican food. Authentic Mexican food is generally a Good Calorie unless it has a high fat content, usually because of excess cheese. It is a classic example of a cuisine in which legumes protect a genetically susceptible population from obesity. Beans form an integral part of many dishes, from burritos to tacos.

Unfortunately, you must be careful in Mexican restaurants because they often add excessive amounts of animal fat to their dishes.

Vegetables. Most vegetables are Good Calories, which is not surprising since they closely resemble our ancestors' preferred diet. The most notable exceptions are carrots and potatoes, which have a high sugar content.

The greatest problem with vegetables is that many people eat them with added fats, such as margarine or butter. By consuming too much fat, you will turn Good Calories into Bad Calories. If you use fat-based spreads, they should be high in unsaturated fats, such as corn oil margarines. Olive oil is *much* better than butter.

BAD CALORIES

The Good Calorie Diet is fundamentally different from conventional diets that limit your caloric intake but allow you to continue to eat your normal selection of low-fat foods. In the Good Calorie Diet, you avoid a few key foods and food combinations, but do not limit calories.

Bad Calories *can* form part of your diet, but only if you combine them with Good Calories (see Chapter 6). For example, carrots are Bad Calories, but they can safely be part of a mixed-vegetable dish. The rules for combining foods are given in Chapter 5.

Many of the foods that you were brought up with are Bad Calories. That is why nutritional diseases are so prevalent in our society. According to Dr Walter C. Willet, chairman of the Department of Nutrition at Harvard School of Public Health, the Western eating pattern is 'probably one of the unhealthiest diets ever to exist on the face of the earth.'[7]

Wheat bread. Common wheat bread is one of the worst Bad Calories. French bread can have twice the fat-forming capacity of sugar. Yet, what is immediately brought to the table when we dine out? A basket of bread. And what do we do? We eat it. By the time our meal arrives, the bread has already raised our blood sugar and insulin, diverting all other food, even Good Calories, into the synthesis of fat. Our appetite also increases. Eliminating bread before meals seems to be one of the easiest paths to quick weight loss.

It does not matter whether it is white-wheat or dark-wheat bread. It is the refining process that makes wheat so fattening. Even whole-wheat flour and health-food wheat breads are Bad Calories if they are finely ground or do not contain the majority of their weight in whole kernels.

If a bread dissolves in your mouth, then it is certainly a Bad Calorie. Oat bread and most barley breads should also be avoided.[8]

One more caution; many bakeries proclaim that their goods are diet products solely because the items are low in fat. Don't be fooled; these baked goods are not acceptable on the Good Calorie Diet. Lowering their fat content does not lower the potential of these products to raise blood sugar; in fact, it can raise their glycaemic index.

Biscuits, cakes and pastries. These products are made with wheat flour and create the same problems as does bread. And, of course, they have large amounts of sugar.

White potatoes. White potatoes have one-third more fat-forming capacity than sugar. Dieters sabotage themselves whenever they eat white potatoes without combining them with Good Calories.

Occasionally, I enjoy a white potato by adding a little olive oil to reduce the glycaemic index. But be careful to do so only when the rest of the meal is low in fat. You do not want to make a high-fat meal even higher in fat.

White potatoes make even more fat when they are processed into instant mashed potatoes. You may think you are avoiding instant potatoes because a product is not labelled as such. However, many restaurants use instant potatoes, and several fast-food chains manufacture their chips from instant potatoes.

And, of course, white potatoes are usually served as

a side dish with animal protein, such as meat, fish and poultry. That combination increases the formation of fat and suppresses appetite controls (see Chapter 6).

Yams and sweet potatoes are Good Calorie alternatives to potatoes, with two-thirds less the fat-forming capacity of white potatoes.

Instant and overcooked rice. Rice is a Good Calorie, but instant rice is a Bad Calorie. Instant rice has twice the fat-forming potential of regular rice. If there is any question as to whether a rice is instant, examine the uncooked grains. If the grains are smooth, they are probably regular rice; if they are rough, they are probably instant.

Overcooking rice can double its fat-forming potential, creating a Bad Calorie. The glutenous rice found in many Chinese restaurants is over-cooked, as is the rice found in many convenience foods, frozen and packaged. These rice dishes are easily identified because the rice grains are not firm and they instantly coagulate into lumpy masses.

When you encounter convenience foods based on rice, it sometimes helps to cook them for less than the recommended time. Then you should examine the cooked product. If the rice grains do not coagulate, your cooking methods have helped it become a Good Calorie.

Rice cakes. Rice cakes are a favourite of dieters, yet they have one of the highest known glycaemic indexes. They form twice the blood sugar of sugar.

Rice drinks. Rice drinks are becoming increasingly popular in health food stores. These drinks are popular because they provide one of the strongest known sugar rushes.

In these drinks processed rice, which already has a

high glycaemic index, is broken down further. The result is a drink that may be one of the worst Bad Calories.

Corn. Modern corn was developed to fatten cattle for market. Therefore, it should be no surprise that corn creates high amounts of blood sugar and fat. Both fresh corn and corn products, such as corn chips and corn flakes, should be avoided.

Just as with white potatoes, I occasionally enjoy corn on the cob with a light coating of olive oil. However, I eat it only when the rest of the meal is low in fat.

Breakfast cereals. A morning bowl of cereal is one of the principal causes of obesity. Most breakfast cereals are made from wheat or corn flour and exhibit the high glycaemic indexes common to these products. Likewise, puffed rice has the same high glycaemic index as rice cakes. Cereals with high glycaemic indexes are why many of us feel so bad in the morning.

Frequently, we follow cereal with an order of eggs, another source of protein. This combination of protein and starch is extremely fattening.

Starting the day with cereal evokes high levels of insulin and ensures that lunch and supper will create extra fat since breakfast has activated your fat-forming enzymes.

Slow-cooked oatmeal appears to be a safe breakfast cereal. But this does not mean that other oat cereals are Good Calories. The food processing involved in converting oats into instant oatmeal, flakes, or other forms of dry cereals raises their glycaemic index to that of sugar. The oats in granola, muesli, and even oat-bran cereals are equally bad; all these cereals have high glycaemic indexes. High fibre bran cereals, however, are generally Good Calories.

In Chapter 5, you will see that without a Good Calorie breakfast, it is nearly impossible to lose weight.

Bananas. Ripe bananas create excess blood sugar and should be avoided.

Canned pasta. Canned pasta has twice the glycaemic index of home-cooked pasta, ranking it among the worst Bad Calorie foods.

Canned soups. You must be careful to choose low-fat soups that do not fall into the following traps. The greatest problem is a high-fat content, so read the label. Also, many companies add food starch, a Bad Calorie, to make their soups thicker. If a canned soup has a substantial pasta or bean content, it probably counts as a Bad Calorie because canning increases the glycaemic index of starches and legumes. Similar problems apply to dehydrated soups.

I have not included an extensive chapter on canned or dehydrated soups, simply because a careful analysis of the glycaemic index of soups is frequently impossible without expensive laboratory measure-ments. That is why many soup recipes are given in Chapter 9.

Dried fruits. Drying fruits concentrates their natural sugars and raises their glycaemic indexes. For example, the glycaemic index of raisins is triple that of grapes. Therefore, you should avoid raisins, dates, dried apples, dried apricots and dried peaches. Soaking dried fruits or nuts does *not* change sub-stantially their glycaemic indexes.

Carrots. Carrots and carrot juice have an extremely high fat-forming potential. They should be avoided – unless as part of a mixed-vegetable dish – in all forms, including raw.

Sugar and honey. Obviously, you should avoid table sugar. What is not so obvious is that honey has a greater fat-forming capacity than sugar.

I wish I could tell you just to substitute artificial sweeteners. Unfortunately, some people have the same insulin reaction to artificial sweeteners as they do to natural ones. To determine if you are susceptible to artificial sweeteners, see if you have the same reactions (lightheadedness, increased appetite, delayed lethargy) to both artificial and naturally sweetened drinks.

When I must use a sweetener, I use sugar. Since I cannot use artificial sweeteners, there is no alternative for me.

Fructose. Fructose is a sugar extracted from fruit. Although it has a low glycaemic index, it can raise the activity of fat-forming enzymes. Therefore, fructose sweetener is a Bad Calorie. Naturally occurring fructose, as found in fruits, is not a Bad Calorie.

Red meat. An important feature of the Good Calorie Diet is that you eat protein and starches or fruit in separate meals. Eat protein early in the day rather than late in the evening. Separate meals containing protein from the next food by several hours. Avoid successive meals that feature protein.

Remember to limit your intake of protein and saturated fat. Since red meats are uniquely high in both protein and saturated fats, you should eat red meat sparingly, not in successive meals. Eat only low-fat meats (see pages 230-32). Most types of beef derive more than 30 per cent of their calories from fat, although some types fall between 31 per cent and 40 per cent and so can be eaten occasionally, according to the diet's guidelines.

Fast foods. Fat, not fast foods, is the enemy. Resist chips and similar goodies. Many fast foods, especially sandwiches, combine protein and starch, which causes them to create extra fat, even if they are low in fat (see Chapter 6). Furthermore, the saturated fat in fast-food meats and deep-fried fish increases the gylcaemic index of the bread in sandwiches.

Tofu. Although soya beans are low on the glycaemic index, the soya bean product tofu is high in fat and should be avoided.

Salads with high-fat salad dressings. High-fat salad dressing is enough to ruin your entire meal. The common ingredients in a green salad – lettuce and tomatoes – have almost no calories. Therefore, the salad dressing determines the majority of the caloric content of the salad. Because most salad dressings are high in fat, they make the entire salad into a Bad Calorie choice.

High-fat salad dressings pose an additional problem – and opportunity. Since they are usually eaten at the beginning of a meal, the fats in salads will affect how you digest the carbohydrates contained in the main courses. If your salad is high in saturated fats, then it is likely to increase the formation of fat. If it is high in unsaturated fats, then it will decrease the fat-forming ability of the rest of the meal. Thus, an olive-oil dressing may actually reduce the fat-forming capacity of the food that follows. Remember that the total fat content of your entire meal must be less than 30 per cent. Therefore, if you start with a fatty salad dressing, then the rest of the meal must be correspondingly low in fat.

Many dieters eat lunches that consist only of salads because salads are low in calories. This is a prime example of how calorie counting can lead you to choose the wrong foods.

Snacks. Most snack foods are high in fat or sugar. Most crisps are Bad Calories because they have both high glycaemic indexes and a high fat content.

Most diets feature in-between-meal snacks in an attempt to prevent the insulin surges common to the Starvation Response. When you need a snack, you should make it a low glycaemic-index fruit.

Alcohol. Preliminary evidence suggests that alcohol will make all other foods behave as if they are Bad Calories. Thus, consuming alcohol before a meal will raise the effective glycaemic index of the whole meal.

Consume all alcohol two to three hours after or before a meal. Avoid drinking alcohol on an empty stomach.

Beer. Beer offers a double whammy. Its calorie content comes from two sources, alcohol and maltose sugar. Maltose has a higher glycaemic index than sugar. The rules for consuming beer are the same as for consuming any other alcoholic beverage.

Sugared soft drinks and juices. Not only do these drinks create high blood sugar levels, but they have far reaching effects on the other foods you eat, making them more fat forming.

Fresh-squeezed juices. Juicing a fruit can raise its glycaemic index. In general, the more pulp left in the juice, the lower the glycaemic index will be. Some juices, such as carrot, beetroot and celery, are almost always Bad Calories.

Juicers create drinks that give you the same sugar rush that you used to get from fizzy drinks.

High-fat foods. You know these foods. They

include salad dressings, many animal products (red meat, dark meat in poultry, most dairy products, and many sweets and chocolates). Don't eat them.

Overcooked foods. Overcooking can double the fat-forming potential of carbohydrates. But not all carbohydrates have an increased glycaemic index after overcooking. Potatoes and rice do, but the thicker forms of spaghetti do not.[9] Avoid overcooking any starchy carbohydrate, since it is not known which ones will have an increased glycaemic index after overcooking.

Just by ordering a food lightly cooked or lightly steamed you can decrease its fat-forming potential.

Instant or processed foods. Remember, the more processed the food, the more blood sugar it makes. Forms of food processing that increase the glycaemic response are precooking and enzymatic digesting to make instant foods, grinding, extruding, flaking and popping.

A good general rule is to avoid any form of processed starchy food.

Popcorn. Popcorn has traditionally been used as an appetite suppressant. However, it has a high glycaemic index and will actually increase your appetite.

Buttering popcorn just increases its glycaemic index. However, adding a little corn-oil spread or olive oil will lower the glycaemic index to acceptable levels. Then your only problem is that you are eating a high-fat snack.

Do not think that this is all the help you will get in selecting Good Calories. To make it easy to choose Good Calories, this book divides foods into Good and Bad Calories (see Chapter 12). The lists include foods from all food groups: meats, poultry, fish, fruit, vegetables, grains and nuts. Chapters 8, 9 and 10 present daily menus, recipes, and restaurant menus. Chapter 5 is also important because it presents the Golden Dozen, rules that are essential for using Good Calories.

5

How to Use Good Calories

HOW TO USE GOOD CALORIES: THE GOLDEN DOZEN

THE GOLDEN DOZEN

The Rules Everyone Must Initially Follow:

1. Eat primarily Good Calories.
2. Combine Good and Bad Calories to make a four-to-one ratio.
3. Eat Good Calorie breakfasts.
4. Eat the most fattening food for lunch, not dinner.
5. Eat Good Calorie snacks.
6. Don't miss a meal.
7. Avoid combining excessive amounts of animal protein with starches and ripe fruit.
8. Avoid excessive amounts of animal products while overcoming the Starvation Response.
9. Avoid the Starvation Response triggers.
10. Avoid vitamin and mineral deficiencies.

Rules to Follow after Overcoming the Starvation Response

11. Eat Good Calories preceding and following Bad Calorie meals.
12. Find your personal limits of freedom.

The Good Calorie Diet is divided into two stages, before and after curing the Starvation Response. The first ten rules serve a dual purpose; they help you counter the Starvation Response and help you lose weight. The last two rules help you eat a wider range of food, but do nothing to help you lose weight. Therefore, it is important to postpone experimenting with the freedoms of the last two rules until you have cured the Starvation Response.

Your first task, as you embark on the Good Calorie Diet, is to embrace the first ten rules. During the first few weeks, you will discover that your body will fight to maintain the Starvation Response. Therefore, during your first few days on the diet, you may experience a suddenly strengthened Starvation Response. Food cravings will grow worse. A few people may experience fluctuations in blood sugar that manifest as minor headaches or lethargy. Do not be alarmed and continue to follow the rules, especially the rule about never missing a meal. Eat frequent snacks. Only by reassuring your body that it does not face starvation can you overcome this last attempt to eat fat-forming foods.

After a few days you will start feeling different, particularly in the morning. During the night your body experiences its longest period without food, so your morning appetite and cravings are mirrors of your state of health. This is why Starvation Response sufferers want to eat Bad Calorie breakfasts, bursting with fatty foods or high-sugar cereals. Once you recover, Good Calorie breakfasts taste better than Bad Calorie ones.

Chapter 8 presents menus that illustrate the principles of this chapter.

THE GOLDEN DOZEN IN DETAIL

1. Eat primarily good calories. It should be no surprise that the first rule of the Good Calorie Diet is to eat a diet that is high in Good Calories. Please note that I did not say that you have to avoid all Bad Calories.

Practical Suggestions: Don't de-emphasize Good Calories once you lose weight. Good Calories may not inhibit the formation of fat in people who are not experiencing the Starvation Response, but this does not mean that they are not still vitally important.

Good Calories are also a preventive medicine. Eating them will prevent you from eating so many Bad Calories that you bring on a new bout of the Starvation Response. Therefore, you should remind yourself that you will always need Good Calories, even after you lose weight. Our genetic inheritance makes them necessary. Good Calories are as essential as is anything else you do to keep yourself healthy.

2. Combine Good and Bad Calories using the four-to-one ratio. Not every food must be a Good Calorie. Your stomach can hide Bad Calories in a mass of lower glycaemic-index food. It is as though you ate a single food with a glycaemic index that is the average of all the foods you consumed. In most cases, that will be the equivalent of a food with a moderate glycaemic index.

Consider this example. If you eat equal calories of carbohydrates with glycaemic indexes of 33 (lentil soup) and 100 (bread), the resulting glycaemic index of the mixture is only 66. The glycaemic index of table sugar – the benchmark – is in the seventies; therefore,

66 is still within the bounds of Good Calorie. When you combine these foods, it is as if you never ate the high glycaemic-index food.

So go ahead and eat Bad Calories, but counter them with Good Calories. You could counter a biscuit with low-fat yogurt or an overly ripe banana with cherries. The possibilities are endless. All you have to do is remember two simple conditions.

First, you must eat both foods at the same time. Averaging glycaemic indexes works only if the foods are consumed at the same time, in the same part of the meal. A Good Calorie main course cannot balance a Bad Calorie appetizer, since the appetizer will boost your blood sugar long before you get to the main course, creating the conditions for the formation of excess fat. Once your hormonal balance is thrown off, all future food, even Good Calorie foods, will make excess fat. Thus, whenever you combine Good and Bad Calories, you should make sure that your first few mouthfuls of food are Good Calories.

Second, you need enough Good Calories to counter the effect of the Bad Calories. The question is, how many Good Calories are needed?

Scientists can compute the average glycaemic index of food combinations by applying a fairly difficult series of equations. I hate doing so. And if I, a trained scientist, find it too much of a hassle to compute these indexes, then I can't expect others to do so.

Instead, I discovered that if you eat four times more Good Calories than Bad Calories, you cannot go wrong. This rule of thumb comes from a simple mathematical truth. Take the worst-case situation, a meal of Good and Bad Calories with glycaemic indexes of 76 (buckwheat) and 131 (French baguette bread), and eat four times more Good Calories than Bad Calories. The glycaemic index of the resulting mixture is 87, barely into the Bad Calorie range. Almost all real-life situations involve foods with lower glycaemic indexes than this hypothetical one; therefore, the four-to-one combination ratio almost always works.

The four-to-one ratio combination works when Good and Bad Calories are combined in the same dish, such as in a casserole or curry, or when they constitute separate dishes, such as bread and mixed vegetables. Either method is a valid way to combine foods as long as you eat the foods at the same time.

Choose from the lists of Good and Bad Calories (in Chapter 12). There is no maths to do or calories to add. You can ignore the numbers associated with the glycaemic index. Everything is simple as long as you eat four times more Good Calories than Bad Calories. There is no need to weigh the food or count calories; just estimate its weight and calories. I know that this method sounds unscientific, but I have found that such seat-of-the-pants estimates are amazingly accurate. You do not have to be exact. If you think you are eating a four-to-one ratio, you are probably safe.

Practical Suggestions: The four-to-one rule applies to combining two or more ingredients in a single dish. Thus, creative cooks can make almost anything into a Good Calorie dish just by adding enough Good Calorie ingredients.

Many ethnic cuisines, including Mexican, Indian, Chinese, Japanese and Italian feature a Good Calorie that is added to almost every main dish. Mexicans add beans; Indians add dhal, a lentil soup; Chinese and

Japanese serve food on rice; and Italians add pasta as a preliminary course before the main dish. These are examples of how people in different cultures develop tricks to keep themselves healthy. These Good Calories balance whatever Bad Calories are served in the same meal.

Becoming accustomed to always having a Good Calorie dish with your meal is a trick that you can emulate. It gives you more freedom. Certainly, it is better to eat a Good Calorie food, rather than the Bad Calorie bread that accompanies so many Western meals.

3. Eat Good Calorie breakfasts. If you eat Good Calorie breakfasts, you will eat less food later in the day, make less blood sugar from the food you eat and inhibit food cravings. Good Calorie breakfasts, such as oatmeal, orange juice, fruit and decaffeinated coffee, are essential to the Good Calorie Diet.

A breakfast of Bad Calories almost doubles the blood sugar produced at lunch 3¾ hours later (see Figure 5-1).[1] Even if you have a Good Calorie lunch, it does not help. The poor breakfast makes the Good Calorie lunch produce the same blood sugar as it would if it were composed of Bad Calories.

This is called 'the second-meal effect,' and it is why breakfast can set the mood for the entire day.[2] If you have a Bad Calorie breakfast, you will probably suffer from the equivalent of a Bad Calorie lunch. The high blood sugar following lunch will then raise your blood sugar at dinner. In other words, a Bad Calorie breakfast can ruin an entire day.

Skipping breakfast is almost as bad. It also raises your blood sugar response to lunch. Therefore, you must eat a Good Calorie breakfast.

There is an additional, and extremely helpful, effect of eating only Good Calorie breakfasts: Good Calories decrease your sense of hunger and minimize the carbohydrate addiction that causes you to choose fatty foods and Bad Calories throughout the day.[3]

One of my friends, John, is a perfect example of how Bad Calorie breakfasts sabotage your entire day. John has set up more than three companies. His car carries not one, but two, cellular telephones. The second phone is cross linked to his portable fax machine, so he can receive and send documents while talking to someone on the first phone. John is on the go from the moment he awakens. It is a rare morning when he stops to eat breakfast. Generally, his secretary brings doughnuts to his desk.

As one would expect, John has a weight problem. I tried to convince him that his basic problem was his breakfast habits. John refused to believe me. He said that the problem was that he craved greasy lunches of hamburgers and chips.

John refused to try the Good Calorie Diet. However, I soon found a backdoor method to experiment on John. When we went on a working holiday in the Caribbean, I insisted on breakfast meetings. Every morning John and I sat down to a feast of fresh fruits and slow-cooked oatmeal.

All our lunches were at the hotel's buffet, which featured everything from greasy meats to pasta. At the beginning of our trip, John would choose the worst Bad Calories for lunch – roast beef, deep-fried shrimp and pastries. I said nothing, curious to see if the Good Calorie breakfasts would take hold. After the first week, I noticed that John had switched to

foods with a lower fat content – primarily grilled fish
– and had stopped eating sweets.

I tried to convince John that the Good Calorie
breakfasts accounted for the difference in his food
preferences at lunch. I failed. John said that it was the
sunshine. He almost convinced me. So I decided to do
another experiment. I cancelled our breakfast meetings. Without the moderating influence of those Good
Calorie breakfasts, it was only a few days before
John's plate was piled with fried foods and sweet
rolls. There was no doubt in my mind: Good Calorie
breakfasts work.

Practical Suggestions: Many people seem to be
addicted to Bad Calorie breakfasts for a simple reason:
they also eat Bad Calorie dinners, and eat them late at
night. These dinners create an abnormal hormonal
flow that alters one's sense of taste in the morning.
Therefore, if you have trouble adjusting to Good
Calorie breakfasts, the first place you should look is at
your evening meals. Change them, and Good Calorie
breakfasts will taste better than Bad Calorie ones.

Some people find that their quest for Good Calories
takes them beyond their traditional concept of
breakfast food. Some Oriental cultures eat rice for
breakfast. Pacific islanders eat fruit. I found that rice
and slow-cooked oatmeal work best for me. It is a
manifestation of modern society that we have come to
think of breakfast as being composed of only Bad
Calorie convenience foods.

FIGURE 5-1

*What Good and Bad Calorie Breakfasts
Do to Postlunch Blood Sugar
(Equal–Calorie Meals)
(Smaller Is Better)*

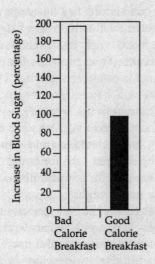

4. Eat the most fat-forming foods for lunch, not for dinner. Eating a big evening meal is one of the worst habits for proper weight loss. At night, our bodies do not remove excess blood sugar but seek to conserve it as a means of ensuring a constant supply of blood sugar while we sleep and cannot eat. So when we eat late in the day, each calorie creates extra fat.

Jack used to work in the computer industry as a programmer. His workday started in the afternoon and lasted until the early hours of the next morning. When Jack went home, he would eat a huge meal and then go to sleep. He was obese. Although he was unwilling to go on a diet, I finally convinced him to eat his large meal at noon, shortly after awakening. It soon became apparent that this simple trick stopped Jack from continuing to gain two pounds every week as he had been doing for the previous six months.

Bad Calorie foods should not be eaten at dinner. Not only do they immediately create extra fat, but they increase the blood sugar that is created after the next morning's breakfast and probably the next lunch as well.[4] So if dinner is composed of animal protein or Bad Calories, you will have a greater appetite and create more fat throughout the next day.

Under ideal conditions, you should eat Good Calorie foods at both breakfast and dinner. That leaves lunch as the optimal time for protein and Bad Calories. Just following this simple rule will make a huge difference in your weight.

The rule against late-night Bad Calories applies to more than dinner. Late-night snacks and alcoholic drinks will also march straight to the nearest fat cell. Since we tend to indulge in these foods well after normal dinner hours, they can be even more devastating than can a Bad Calorie dinner. If you are up late at night and want a snack, make sure it is a Good Calorie snack, such as fruit. Avoid all foods that contain or will make excess fat.

What are the consequences of violating these rules? A University of Minnesota study, published in the proceedings of the Tenth International Congress on Nutrition, showed that people gained weight when fed a diet late in the day and lost weight when fed the same diet at breakfast. With a 2,000 calorie diet, the difference between the two groups was an amazing 2.3 pounds per week.

These studies were so startling that scientists repeated them. Instead of a set diet, participants could eat whatever they wanted in a single meal. There were no calorie limitations. One group ate breakfast within one hour of rising. Another group ate after 6 p.m. The result was that the breakfast group had a weight-loss advantage of 1.8 pounds per week.

Practical Suggestions: This rule is practically tailor-made for those who must eat out for lunch. Since lunch is when you should eat protein or other Bad Calories, choosing from a restaurant menu is fairly easy.

There's no doubt that it can be troublesome to eat Good Calorie dinners at restaurants. But there are always good choices, especially pasta and vegetables – skip the cream sauces. Since restaurants are in the business of selling food, they will try to sell the maximum amount of food at dinner, especially the more expensive main courses that feature animal protein. It is important to be strong and limit your intake of Bad Calories and animal protein. If you order a dinner that includes these items, eat sparingly while filling up on salad and vegetables. Take home a doggie bag of the excess food.

For many of us, dinner has become the prime forum for intimacy and the expression of love. Lovers or the family gather together for the evening meal. If your love relationship or family has been oriented around these principles, then you must gain a consensus as to your proposed change in eating habits. Dinner can still be a large meal. The only difference is that it will be composed of Good Calories.

If you must have your large meal in the evening, it does not mean that you cannot lose weight. It will just be more difficult to do so. However, you should try to have nothing but Good Calorie evening meals that do not feature animal products.

5. Eat Good Calorie snacks. Eating more frequently reduces insulin, blood sugar and fat in the blood.[5] This is how our ancestors ate as they foraged for food; only when they started to hunt did they eat a single big meal. If you get hungry between meals, you should eat Good Calorie snacks.

You do not have to snack, but it will give you more latitude during meals. The lower the glycaemic index of the snack, the more it aids the digestion of future meals.

Practical Suggestions: Fruit is a great snack. So is fat-free bean dip.

Obviously you should avoid Bad Calorie snacks, such as crisps, corn chips, sweets, hamburgers and chips.

6. Don't miss a meal. Never starve yourself. It is the one thing guaranteed to induce the Starvation Response. Just a few days of starvation can increase your fat-forming potential more than fourfold. Skipping a single meal can change your brain biochemistry and make you eat fattening foods in future meals.

Practical Suggestions: Although this would seem to be an easy rule, it goes against the long experience of most habitual dieters. Whereas conventional diets make you eat less, the Good Calorie Diet works by making you choose the proper foods while eating fully. You must remind yourself that your job is not to punish your body but to make it feel comfortable.

If you cannot eat a full meal, you should make sure that you have several Good Calorie snacks, each a few hours apart. The ingestion of Good Calories will, via the second-meal effect, decrease your response to future meals.

7. Avoid combining excessive amounts of animal protein with starchy carbohydrates or fruit. This is a case in which red meats, poultry, fish and dairy products all create the same problem. Combining anything that creates large amounts of blood sugar, such as starches or fruits, with animal protein inhibits the enzyme that places excess blood sugar into glycogen storage, thus elevating blood sugar and insulin levels and diverting large amounts of blood sugar into triglyceride fats.[6]

Figure 5-2 shows that combining protein with white potatoes or spaghetti almost doubles the peak insulin response.[7] It also shows that animal protein will increase the fat-forming potential of both Good and Bad Calorie carbohydrates. Spaghetti is a Good Calorie, and white potatoes are Bad Calories. Yet the increase in insulin is roughly equal when either is combined with animal protein. This is one of the few cases in which Good Calories cannot prevent the formation of excess fat. Part of the problem is the saturated fat in animal proteins.

The combination of starch and animal protein also causes us to overeat because it inhibits the release of glucagon, the enzyme that signals when our stomachs are full.[8]

I have already mentioned that bread is one of the worst Bad Calories. Now, you can see that the fat-forming potential of bread is further enhanced if it is included in meat sandwiches. Hamburgers, even low-fat hamburgers, can never be Good Calories. The same admonition applies to fish sandwiches, such as tuna.

Pizza appears to be an acceptable food, one that should cause no problems as long as it does not have meat toppings. Cheese topping, used in moderation, contains so little protein that it does not evoke the problems outlined in this section. Of course, you should use low-fat cheese or normal cheese in sufficient moderation that less than 30 per cent of the calories come from fat.

While I was writing this book, I decided to test what would happen if I combined excessive amounts of animal protein and starches. I had already cured the Starvation Response, and my weight was low. I ate animal protein with mashed potatoes. For four days nothing happened, and then the Starvation Response appeared. Within two weeks I had gained eight pounds.

Not wanting to carry the experiment too far, I began to eat meals with no animal protein, but that change was not enough. Until I returned to a diet of Good Calories, thereby thwarting the Starvation Response, my weight did not return to normal.

Combining animal protein and starch gave me a clear message, and it will do the same for you. When you are suffering from the Starvation Response, vegetable proteins are better because they do not create excess fat when combined with starches or fruit.

When eating animal protein, combine it with either salads or vegetables that don't have as much potential to raise your blood sugar. You can also eat animal

FIGURE 5-2

*Increases in Peak Insulin When Protein
Is Combined with Carbohydrates
(Smaller Is Better)*

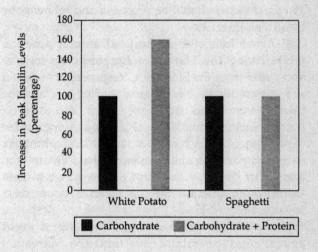

protein with meals in which starch or fruit predominate if you limit your intake of animal protein.
It's simple.

Finally, do not interpret this rule to mean that you
should totally avoid either protein or carbohydrates.
Both are fine foods. Just have them in separate meals.

Practical Suggestions: Don't panic; this rule is not as
restrictive as it seems at first. You can have meat-
based sauces with spaghetti and clams with linguine.
The key is that the protein must be a minor part of the

meal. Thus, if you eat grilled fish as the main course, so the meal is mainly protein, then do not have white potatoes or rice as a side dish.

After the Starvation Response has subsided, you can eat sandwiches. However, you should realize that they are Bad Calories and treat them as such (see Rule 11). Sandwiches should be preceded and followed by Good Calorie meals.

8. Avoid excessive amounts of animal products while curing the Starvation Response. As long as you suffer from the Starvation Response, you should not eat meals in which animal products are the primary ingredients. Ingesting animal flesh turns off the normal mechanisms of energy storage, the deposition of energy in muscle and liver glycogen, and switches to mechanisms that create fat. Remember that only two days of eating high-protein foods or unsaturated fat can increase your blood sugar over fourfold.

This rule does not mean that you have to avoid animal products totally. But until the Starvation Response vanishes, you should eat low-fat animal products only as side dishes. For example, you can add small amounts to pasta sauce, a little tuna to a salad, or a few ounces of chicken to a meal that features Good Calorie vegetables and fruit.

During this period, avoid animal products that are high in saturated fat, such as red meat. Chicken and turkey are better than red meat, but still have more saturated fats than do some fish.

Don't be concerned about eating less protein. Our protein needs are much less than we may think. The World Health Organization estimates that people need a half gram of protein per kilogram of body weight, meaning that a 10 stone person needs 30 grams of protein per day (6 ounces of fish, 4 ounces of beefsteak, or 4 ounces of cheese). Others estimate that we need no more than 20 grams per day.[9]

Several lines of evidence suggest that we are healthier when we eat less protein. The average Westerner consumes over 100 grams of protein per day, which contributes to obesity, diabetes and osteoporosis.[10] Seventh Day Adventists, a vegetarian religious group, have lower rates of cancer and heart disease and live longer.

I don't expect all readers to eliminate animal products from their diets permanently. In fact, such a practice may be counterproductive. Serotonin, the neurotransmitter that controls appetite and cravings, measures the balance between sugar and protein in the bloodstream. When either substance is disproportionately low, serotonin makes you crave it. When you eat Bad Calorie carbohydrates, the resulting rise in blood sugar makes it seem as though you have eaten an enormous quantity of carbohydrates; therefore, you'll crave protein. After you overcome the Starvation Response, your blood sugar will return to normal, and you will need less protein to maintain the balance.

If you find that you crave protein when you eat no animal products, eat a little animal protein. However, be careful not to pay attention to this craving until you have been following the first ten rules for several weeks. The avoidance of animal protein during this period allows your body to overcome the artificial needs imposed by the Starvation Response.

Practical Suggestions: Vegetable proteins should be a mixture of legumes (beans) and grains in a ratio of 1 to 2^1/$_2$, for example, 2^1/$_2$ parts rice to 1 part beans. This mixture will provide all the amino acids necessary for building muscle. The process of combining different vegetables is called protein complementation. Until recently, it was thought that both legumes and grains had to be eaten in the same meal, but some scientists now say that the two foods can be eaten in different meals. I have not had any problem eating a diet that does not always combine legumes and grains in the same meal.

Some people may experience intestinal gas until they become accustomed to their new diet. If this happens to you, you may wish to take pills that are designed to help with this problem. Don't worry. The discomfort is only temporary, and your digestive muscles will soon become accustomed to transporting Good Calorie foods.

9. Avoid the Starvation Response Triggers. Chapter Three discussed the conditions that increase the fat-forming potential of all food, even Good Calories. They are repeated here. Keep them in mind.

AVOID THINGS THAT INCREASE FAT FORMATION

Avoid foods that are high in fat.

Avoid saturated fats; substitute unsaturated fats.

Avoid overcooked carbohydrates.

Avoid overly ripe fruit.

Avoid processed foods.

Avoid canned starches and legumes.

Avoid fructose.

Avoid alcohol before a meal.

Avoid smoking before a meal.

Avoid bad calories before and during exercise.

10. Avoid vitamin and mineral deficiencies. Humans evolved to eat plants that are rich in vitamins and minerals. In times of starvation, one of the signals of the need to create excess fat was vitamin and mineral deficiencies. Today, such deficiencies are strongly associated with the Starvation Response, whose victims excrete significantly more, and absorb fewer, vitamins and minerals than non-sufferers.[11] Therefore, if you are experiencing the Starvation Response, a normal, well-balanced diet is not enough; you must take vitamin and mineral supplements.

Vitamin C. The Starvation Response induces Vitamin C deficiencies.[12] When you lack Vitamin C, blood sugar does not become glycogen and is thus made available for forming fat.[13] You also need Vitamin C for the proper release of insulin.[14]

Vitamin D. Levels of vitamin D are much lower in people with the Starvation Response.[15] You should be concerned because Vitamin D deficiencies may cause the abnormal regulation of blood sugar.[16]

Vitamin E. Vitamin E supplementation decreases blood sugar.[17]

Magnesium. Magnesium deficiencies have been linked to insulin resistance, a primary symptom of the Starvation Response.[18]

Potassium. In non-sufferers of the Starvation Response, insulin stimulates the entry of potassium into the liver and muscles, where blood sugar is converted into glycogen.[19] With the Starvation Response however, insulin loses its ability to stimulate the uptake of potassium.[20]

Copper. The average person is likely to have a copper deficiency.[21] Copper supplements lower the triglyceride levels of copper-deficient people who are experiencing the Starvation Response by more than 70 per cent, but do nothing for non-sufferers with the same copper deficiency.[22]

Unfortunately, fructose aggravates a copper deficiency, and the combination of a copper deficiency and a high-fructose diet increases the risk of heart attacks in men.[23]

Chromium. Many people are so deficient in chromium that the normal regulation of blood sugar is nearly impossible.[24] Food processing, Bad Calories, and caloric restriction all induce chromium deficiencies that elevate blood sugar, insulin, insulin resistance, cholesterol, and triglycerides.[25] Chromium supplements counteract these problems.[26]

Only a handful of modern foods contain significant quantities of chromium. They include brewer's yeast, beer, black pepper, liver, lobsters, oysters, mushrooms, shrimps and whole grains.

Almost nobody can live on a diet of these foods, although I once watched a friend try. He was about to be fired from his job and wanted to charge his company for outlandish meals. I know it sounds bizarre, but every day he ate at least five lobsters and washed them down with the finest imported beers. At the end of the week he dreaded the moment he would step on the scales. To his complete amazement, he had not gained any weight. Rather, he had lost five pounds. Although seafood restaurants may love it, I am not about to write *The Lobster and Beer Miracle Diet*. It is not healthy. I suspect, however, that this certainly shows what can happen when you get enough chromium.

You should take chromium supplements, but chromium must be in a special form before it will do anything in the body. Chromium picolinate has received massive publicity, but numerous authorities have questioned whether it is effective or even safe.[27] Of the many chromium supplements that are available, chromium-polynicotinic acid complexes appear to be the most active, producing a 15 per cent decrease in blood sugar, a 20 per cent to 30 per cent decrease in cholesterol, and decreased triglycerides.[28]

Recommended Supplements: To counter any vitamin or mineral deficiencies while you're on the Good Calorie Diet, I recommend that you take the following supplements: 200 mcg of chromium-polynicotinate, 300 mg of vitamin C, the RDA of vitamin B complex and the RDA of vitamin D and good mineral tablets (with at least the minimum recommended daily allowance of calcium, zinc, potassium and magnesium). You also need 3 mg of copper if you eat fructose, especially if you are a man.

BEFORE YOU ENJOY THE FREEDOM OF THE LAST TWO RULES, DETERMINE WHEN YOU HAVE OVERCOME THE STARVATION RESPONSE

Until you overcome the Starvation Response, a process that should take fewer than two weeks, you do not have the freedom to relax the first ten rules of the Good Calorie Diet. To figure out when you can relax the rules, examine the list of symptoms of the Starvation Response. Compare the symptoms to the symptoms you experienced before you went on the Good Calorie Diet. If several have disappeared, then you have probably overcome the Starvation Response and are ready to move on. For most people, observing the first ten rules for two weeks is enough to do the trick.

Remember, the symptoms are as follows:

SYMPTOMS OF THE STARVATION RESPONSE

1. Regular over-eating.
2. Eating rapidly.
3. Difficulty knowing when one's stomach is full.
4. Strong or persistent hunger.
5. Craving high-fat or high-sugar food.
6. Occasional binge eating.
7. Snacking at night.
8. Gaining weight on less food.
9. Regaining weight easily.
10. Gaining weight after a pregnancy or while taking either birth control or oestrogen-replacement pills.

If you still exhibit a majority of the symptoms after two weeks, then you should re-examine your activities. Are you following the dietary instructions properly? Have you eaten protein-rich or high-fat meals? Are you snacking inappropriately? Do you still drink alcohol before a meal or on an empty stomach? Do you drink too much alcohol? If you look long enough, you will find what you are doing wrong and can easily correct it.

If you determine that your symptoms have subsided, then you are free to move on to the last two rules. They help you to select the greatest variety of foods that your genetics will allow. They may allow you to eat Bad Calorie meals and other junk foods while still losing weight.

During the first several weeks after you have cured the Starvation Response, follow the suggestions in Chapter 8 on how often to have meals containing animal proteins. During this time, the stress of introducing animal proteins makes them count as Bad Calorie meals. Treat them as such and avoid other Bad Calorie meals.

11. Good Calorie meals should precede and follow Bad Calorie meals. After you have cured the Starvation Response, you can enjoy Bad Calorie meals. To avoid re-evoking the Starvation Response, you should make sure that you precede and follow Bad Calorie meals with two days of Good Calorie meals. If you have been eating Good Calorie meals for the past few days, then your body will not over-react if you eat a Bad Calorie meal. Similarly, a few days of Good Calorie meals will normalize your system after a Bad Calorie meal.

Avoid eating any more food, either Good or Bad Calories, while digesting a Bad Calorie meal or snack. If you wait long enough for your next meal, then you will make less fat.

How long do you have to wait before the wrong enzymes subside? You have already seen that $3^3/4$ hours is too short a time (see Rule 3); however, by $5^3/4$ hours after a Bad Calorie breakfast the second-meal effect has dissipated.[29] So, simply wait six hours before eating the next meal. This rule does not mean that you have to wait six hours between *all* meals, just after a Bad Calorie meal. If you cannot wait six hours, then wait at least five hours.

Felicia is a magazine editor. She claims to have read

more than a hundred diet books and certainly knows about conventional diets. When she read an early version of the Good Calorie Diet, she was filled with questions about why my advice was so different from conventional diets. After she read the manuscript, our first phone calls were filled with her scepticism. Then she went on holiday. Naturally, she went to a good restaurant and had a fat-filled lunch. Remembering my rule, she waited six hours before having dinner. The next day, she phoned me and was full of excitement. Ordinarily, the large lunch would have made her ravenously hungry at dinner. But after waiting six hours, she was *less* hungry than normal. Several times she tried this trick, and it always worked. Then, and only then, did she decide to try the rest of the Good Calorie Diet.

Practical Suggestions: While you are curing the Starvation Response, your meals will not include animal sources of protein. You avoid animal protein to reassure your body that it does not face starvation. After you have cured the Starvation Response, you should *gradually* reintroduce animal protein into your diet, if that is your nutritional preference. Remember, you do not have to eat animal protein, but neither do you have to avoid it.

While you are gradually reintroducing your body to animal protein, remember that meals with animal products count as Bad Calorie meals. Therefore, you must initially precede and follow them with several days of Good Calorie meals. Later you can introduce more meals containing animal products until you are eating them every other day. Remember that if you start to re-experience the symptoms of the Starvation

Response, you should immediately discontinue whatever form of Bad Calories you are eating, including animal products. Fortunately, this is a rare response, and most people can tolerate some animal products.

After you have become reaccustomed to eating animal protein without evoking the Starvation Response, then these meals no longer count as Bad Calories. That is why low-fat animal proteins are listed as being Good Calories. After you have stabilized your intake of animal products at your desired level for two weeks, then you can try substituting meals that contain other forms of Bad Calories. Chapter 8 contains meal plans that illustrate these principles.

Remember, you can minimize the effects of discretionary Bad Calories by eating them at lunch, rather than at dinner. This suggestion is critical for eating animal protein. Lunch is the only time when you should subject your body to that stress.

You can prepare for a forthcoming party by eating nothing but Good Calorie meals for several days, to normalize your system. Then you can enjoy Bad Calories at the party. Afterwards, you should eat nothing but Good Calorie meals for several days.

While recovering from a Bad Calorie meal, you should also remember that Good Calorie meals can include Bad Calories via the four-to-one rule. There is no reason to be unnecessarily hard on yourself.

Finally, you should never atone for junk-food binges with caloric restriction. A Bad Calorie meal followed by starvation is the classic signal to initiate the Starvation Response. In short, a Bad Calorie lunch is better than a Bad Calorie dinner. If you have a Bad

Calorie lunch, you can compensate for it with a Good Calorie dinner. Eating a Bad Calorie dinner means that you must wait overnight before eating again, and that is too long a time to go without food.

12. After curing the Starvation Response, find your personal limits of freedom. If you want to enjoy the maximum freedom, then you must experiment because the Starvation Response emerges differently in each person. I can give a list of rules that will work for everybody, but that list will include rules that you do not need. Different people are sensitive to different aspects of the Good Calorie Diet. For example, I am most sensitive to proper mineral supplementation. The wife of a good friend of mine is most sensitive to alcohol before meals. My daughter appears to be intolerant of excessive fat in her food.

After you are losing weight on a regular basis, you can slowly push the bounds of dietary freedom and occasionally enjoy a sinfully delicious meal that goes against the principles you learned in this book. Months later, you will be able to do so more often. A good rule is to explore alternative meals once a week after you have been on the diet for three months and twice a week during the following month.

If you go too far in your experiments, the Starvation Response will begin to reappear. You will stop losing weight or crave unusual foods and develop a larger appetite. When that happens, you should celebrate, for you now have one of the most valuable pieces of information – knowledge of what it takes for your body to become ill. You know exactly how much freedom you can enjoy without worrying.

Practical Suggestions: Remember, the operative word in

the previous paragraphs is *slowly*. If you have just overcome the Starvation Response, you also have to be careful not to violate the other rules of The Good Calorie Diet. Later, after you've established a healthy state, you can *gradually* expand the boundaries of your explorations.

Our bodies are in the same situation as in a small child awakening from a nightmare. As we comfort our bodies, we must train them to do nothing that reintroduces the fear and panic that lurks just below the surface. We much teach our bodies to recognize that occasional Bad Calories are not a sign of impending starvation.

Only time will tell you your limits. Sometimes you may go too far. Your body may have a greater or lesser tolerance for cheating. The only way to know is to experiment – slowly and sanely.

To lose weight, all you have to do is limit yourself to the first ten rules of this section. At some point, you will find that the symptoms of the Starvation Response have disappeared, and you can then expand your freedom somewhat. As long as you stay within the limits that apply to you, you will lose weight.

DAILY AND RESTAURANT MENUS

So how do you incorporate The Golden Dozen Rules into your daily life? To make your job easier, Chapter 8 presents two sets of daily menus, one to use while combating the Starvation Response and one for afterwards. Clearly, you can use the menus designed to combat the Starvation Response even after you have overcome that condition. In addition, Chapter 10

helps you to eat in American, Chinese, fast-food,
French, Italian, Japanese, Mexican and seafood
restaurants. Of course, the main problem with listing
restaurant menus is that the recipes vary. So use these
menus as a guide, not as absolute rules. They are also
a good guide for home menus.

6

What to do if you do not lose weight

ARE YOU FOLLOWING THE PROGRAMME?

The Good Calorie Programme works, without modifications, for the vast majority of people who experience the Starvation Response. It will not make you look like a 12-year-old underfed youngster, but it will restore you to a healthy body without excessive concentrations of fat.

But what if it does not work for you? There may be medical reasons, but before you start looking for them, you should ask yourself one question: did I follow the programme?

Jackie Alexander is a 35-year-old hospital administrator, who exercises regularly and exudes good health. I first met her in the gym. She walked up to me and said that she heard I had developed an amazing weight-loss programme. She was five feet five and overweight; she wanted to lose a stone. When she went on the Good Calorie Diet she did not lose weight. Three weeks later she approached me and informed me that my diet was a failure. I spent the next half hour with her going over everything she ate. At first I was mystified. Then I discovered that she consumed several high-protein, high-sugar shakes after each exercise session. When I told her that drinking these shakes violated the rule against consuming protein combined with excess blood sugar, she was astonished. In her mind 'protein' meant a piece of meat or fish on a plate.

Jackie stopped drinking the protein shakes and devoted herself to overcoming the Starvation Response. After ten days she started to lose two pounds per week. Within a few months she reached her target weight. Jackie was thrilled. She had been promoted at work and thought that her image was the deciding factor. While I prefer to think that her competence earned her the promotion, I was pleased that her weight loss had given her a psychological edge that might have helped.

Some people, like Jackie, find it hard to follow the rules. They have some habit that is so deeply ingrained that they do not think about it. Many people are so accustomed to their pre-dinner alcoholic drinks that they allow this habit to persist even though it raises their blood sugar. Other people work late and eat dinner very late in the evening; it will be difficult for them to lose weight. Some people still mix protein and starchy carbohydrates, especially when they eat in restaurants and potatoes or rice are served as a side dish.

And there are always the anxious people who engage in Bad Calorie meals before they have cured the Starvation Response. It is important to complete the first ten rules of the Golden Dozen presented in Chapter Five before relaxing the programme. If you enjoy the freedom of potentially fat-forming foods prematurely, you must start again from the beginning.

Another common problem is that some people think that the Good Calorie Diet's freedom means that they can engage in gluttony. Following a diet that does not restrict the quantity of food does not mean you can behave as if you are at a Roman orgy. If you are overeating, slow down and realize that it induces the Starvation Response.

Some people will need to combine exercise with weight loss. These are the people who suffer from a double problem – they make too much fat and they burn too little fat. However, *fewer* people than one would think require vigorous exercise for weight loss once they overcome the Starvation Response. *Do not* automatically assume that exercise is necessary for weight loss. However, don't ignore the benefits of exercise for general conditioning and cardiovascular health.

STRESS CAN AGGRAVATE THE STARVATION RESPONSE

When you suffer from the Starvation Response, you are at war with yourself. Insulin and high blood sugar send abnormal signals to your brain and alter more than your appetite. Like anyone whose body is at war with itself, you suffer from abnormal stress that pervades every thought. To be healthy, you must undo the damage that the Starvation Response has done to your mental health.

Mental stress has numerous measurable effects, many of which strengthen the Starvation Response. During mental stress, fat cells are activated, so that more blood circulates through them and more blood sugar flows within them, maximizing the formation of fat.[1] Furthermore, blood sugar is routed away from pathways that would burn it. Mental stress also alters the activity of the sympathetic nervous system, the same system that helps determine appetite and food preferences.[2] Finally, stress increases the secretion of glucocorticoid, which promotes a response that closely resembles that seen in starvation.[3]

Mental stress also severs the connection between your mind and your body, making it difficult to listen to the messages that ordinarily control your eating patterns. More than appetite controls, these messages contain the intelligence of your body, the same intelligence that will steer you to the proper combinations of Good and Bad Calories.

The bottom line is that mental stress creates a deadly positive feedback loop that locks you into the formation of excess fat. The Starvation Response creates mental stress, and that stress strengthens the Starvation Response, which, in turn, creates more stress.

The way out of these problems is to reduce your levels of physical and mental stress. Some people find that exercise helps relieve stress, whereas others engage in meditation. Whatever technique you choose, you will find that lowering stress can frequently provide the last needed bit of momentum to overcome the Starvation Response.

PERSISTENT CASES OF THE STARVATION RESPONSE

Suppose you are eating reasonably, exercising, and following the rules, but you are still not losing weight. The first thing to do is see your doctor to make sure that your weight problem is not a symptom of a serious disease. If you find that you are in good health, you should realize that you suffer from a special form of the Starvation Response.

A small percentage of people, unfortunately, can never rid themselves of the Starvation Response. Their bodies are so strongly programmed that Bad Calories will always evoke the Starvation Response. For these people, there is a simple solution: follow the first ten rules of the Golden Dozen in Chapter Five, but not the last two.

If you suspect that you are among this group, practise these first ten rules for five weeks. If you lose weight during that time, then continue on to the next two rules. If you stop losing weight at that point, return to and continue to follow only the first ten rules. Although the first ten rules are more stringent, you should find relief in the knowledge that you will lose weight while following them.

People who have to lose more than 4 stone are another exception. They have a special set of problems. Not only will they have to remain within the bounds of the first ten rules, but they frequently have to decrease the amount of foods they eat because they suffer from other forms of excess fat formation and decreased fat burning, in addition to the Starvation Response. They are the *only* people who should follow the rules of the next section.

COMBINING GOOD CALORIES AND CALORIC RESTRICTION

I do not normally recommend caloric restriction as a method of weight loss, but the experience of my

friend George taught me the value of Good Calories in
such a programme.

George used to weigh over 28 stone. He had to
modify his car, so he could fit into the driver's seat.
His clothes were like bags, hanging over a mass of
flesh that he could barely move. George wanted to
follow the Good Calorie Diet, but there was no time.
His doctor said that George's health was at risk and
that he had to lose huge amounts of weight
immediately. I knew that this would not be possible in
six months on the Good Calorie Diet. Such a drastic
loss of weight is medically inadvisable except under a
doctor's direct, and constant, supervision. Therefore,
George and I decided to try an experiment. He would
restrict himself to 1,250 calories a day of the Good
Calories with the lowest glycaemic indexes (see
Chapter 11) and would also follow the first ten rules of
the Golden Dozen.

George liked the combination of caloric restriction
and Good Calories because he could eat a greater
volume of food; 1,250 calories a day felt more like
2,000 or 3,000. However, I did not expect much from
the combination of caloric restriction and Good
Calories. To my surprise, Good Calories prevented
many of the food cravings and irritability that
normally accompany caloric restriction. However, it
was clear that George still suffered from the
Starvation Response. He would experience hunger
and excess blood sugar whenever he ate any Bad
Calories.

George lost weight fairly rapidly – more rapidly
than he had with liquid shakes and starvation. I
remember the day he proudly showed me his new car.
It was showroom perfect and completely unmodified.

I do not know how much weight he lost, but it was well in excess of 7 stone.

When it was obvious that George's diet was coming to an end, I waited anxiously to see how much weight he would regain. Since he was suffering from a controlled case of the Starvation Response, I suggested that he devote himself to overcoming the Starvation Response by limiting himself to the first ten rules of the Good Calorie Diet. Perhaps immediately attacking the Starvation Response would prevent him from once again requiring a custom car.

Overcoming the Starvation Response was a pleasure for George. It was just like his old diet except that he could eat more food. Every time I saw George, he would smile and tell me how many second helpings of food he had enjoyed.

We extended the diet to six months and then *very gradually* introduced many of the freedoms of the last two rules. He regained a few pounds, but so few that his report was my only clue.

I was curious: was this success a generalized phenomenon, or was it something unique to George? I tried a modified form of George's diet with Ann and Jill, both of whom were impatient to lose weight. Instead of 1,000 calories, they ate 1,500 calories a day. Other than that, they followed the same restrictions as did George. In two months, Ann lost 1 stone 4 pounds, and Jill lost 1 stone 7 pounds. However, this is where their stories diverge.

Ann's goal had been to look good in a bathing suit because she was going on a Caribbean holiday. She did nothing to prevent the Starvation Response while on holiday. In two weeks she regained over a stone.

Jill stayed in town and worked on overcoming the

Starvation Response. She then spent another two months gradually easing into the freedom of the last two rules. After four months she had regained only two pounds. She looked great and felt great.

These case histories illustrate the possibilities and traps of restricting food while eating Good Calories. You will lose weight faster, but you will suffer from a greater case of the Starvation Response. Without the *strictest* recovery periods, you will regain every pound. You must stick to only the first ten rules. Because Ann never took the time to prevent the Starvation Response, she regained every pound. Jill took the time, and she is still slim.

Though I am generally pretty easygoing about violating the rules, I am now going to sound like a drill sergeant addressing new recruits. If you go on a caloric-restriction diet, you should not break the first ten rules for at least *six months* after you start to restrict calories. The last two rules are no longer operative. You cannot eat unaccompanied Bad Calories. You can not cheat if you want to lose weight and not regain it.

When you do follow caloric restrictions, be sure to consult Chapter 11 and eat only the foods with the lowest glycaemic indexes. Although these foods will not provide as much of a taste treat, they will provide the maximum volume of foods.

Who should attempt to combine caloric restriction with the nutritional principles of the Good Calorie Diet? Obviously, people who have a lot of weight to lose. This combination will also work for people who must lose weight quickly.

I do *not* recommend caloric restriction for people who need to lose only a couple of stone. The normal

Good Calorie Diet is much more sensible, does not present the enormous threat of rebound weight gains, is easier to implement, and is more forgiving of deviations. It is also much faster in the sense that you spend less time thinking about strict food restrictions. I lost 2 stone in just a few months on the normal programme. Others have lost up to 4 stone in less than a year.

I am not totally opposed to combining food restriction and Good Calories, especially since some scientists have suggested that malnutrition and other medical emergencies make the Starvation Response irreversible.[4] Those who experience an irreversible Starvation Response will not lose weight only by following the first ten rules of the Golden Dozen. They, and only they, should follow this programme.

Using caloric restriction unnecessarily is like amputating your hands to cure hangnails. It will cure the problem, but it will create long-term consequences that are unnecessary. Most readers should enjoy the freedom of eating fully and losing weight without caloric restriction.

7

The Good Calorie Solution

GOOD CALORIES THWART THE STARVATION RESPONSE

Good Calories are the only sure way to overcome the Starvation Response. I have already presented many examples of how Bad Calories boost and Good Calories counter the Starvation Response. Chapters Two and Three reviewed many scientific studies that have found that Good Calories reverse insulin resistance, lower blood sugar, and inhibit the synthesis of triglycerides, and many other studies have found the same results.[1]

Only one month of a Good Calorie diet decreases concentrations of triglycerides.[2] HDL triglycerides, the form of fat that moves into fat cells, are cut in half by Good Calories (see Figure 7-1 in Appendix 1).

Good Calories lower triglycerides almost as effectively as cloibrate, a drug developed for that purpose.[4] Yet Good Calories are much safer than drugs that have the potential to cause gallstones, cancer and other adverse effects.[5]

Several studies have examined the effects of Good Calories on diabetic patients whose blood sugar is much more out of control than is that of people who are experiencing the Starvation Response. Therefore, diabetic patients would seem to be in the worst possible situation to test the effect of Good Calories, yet Good Calories still have a positive effect on them. Only two weeks of Good Calories lowered the blood sugar of diabetic patients by 29 per cent.[6] After five weeks on a low glycaemic-index diet, their triglycerides decreased 20 per cent.[7]

GOOD CALORIES LOWER APPETITE AND REVERSE CRAVINGS FOR BAD CALORIES

Good Calories change your brain biochemistry, so you want to eat less food.[9] In a pioneering study, Brand gave subjects six different breakfasts that contained foods that ranged from 43 to 116 on the glycaemic index.[10] The higher the glycaemic index of a food, the less it satisfied the subjects' hunger. Conversely, the lower the glycaemic index, the more the food satisfied their hunger.

Good Calories not only reduce your present hunger, but decrease your food intake by allowing a longer time to pass before you become hungry again. When people eat shepherd's pie prepared with beans, rather than with white potatoes, for example, there is a significant difference in the time it takes for them to get hungry again.[11] Just eating a few Good Calorie snacks produces a spontaneous decrease in the consumption of food by 150 fewer calories per day.[12] If you eat Good Calories for breakfast, you will spontaneously eat less during lunch, but still feel totally satisfied.[13] Good Calorie carbohydrates reduce your appetite by reversing the insulin and serotonin abnormalities that cause you to crave food.[14]

GOOD CALORIES INCREASE FAT BURNING

The Starvation Response, malnutrition and excess blood sugar all decrease the rate at which fat burns, thereby allowing your body to hoard energy stored as fat.[15] Because your body is sensitive to the ratio of fat to blood sugar produced from food, extremely low-fat or high blood-sugar diets comprised of Bad Calories can decrease your metabolic set-point. In contrast, lowering blood sugar increases the rate of fat burning.[16]

Therefore, you do not give up the metabolic advantages of conventional diets when you pursue the Good Calorie Diet. I like to think that this diet combines the best of both worlds.

MILLIONS HAVE USED GOOD CALORIES

Scientists have studied representative samples of millions of people who are overweight when they eat Bad Calories and thin when they eat Good Calories. Their stories gave me the idea for the Good Calorie Diet.

Scientific studies have found that Native Americans, Australian Aborigines, Alaskan Eskimos, African Zulus, Asian Indians, Mexicans, and Yemenite Jews are overweight and diabetic on Bad Calories, but quickly lose both weight and excess blood sugar when they eat Good Calories. The correlation between blood sugar and weight is best seen in the Pima Indians of Arizona.

The Pima originally lived in the arid desert valleys of Arizona and worked farms built around an elaborate system of irrigation canals.[17] Their diet consisted of low glycaemic-index carbohydrates: acorn stew, mesquite cakes made from cacti, corn hominy made from low-sugar corn, tepary beans and lima beans. It is a diet that induces lower levels of blood sugar than any other commonly used diet.[18]

The Pima abandoned their original diet a century ago when white settlers appropriated their farmlands and water. Living on reservations, they ate surplus wheat flour, sugar, coffee, processed cereals and lard. Although this diet sounds crude, it consists of about the same percentages of fat, protein, and carbohydrate that are found in the typical Western diet. Unfortunately, it also induces high blood-sugar levels.

The Pima soon grew obese with their new diet. On some reservations three-quarters of the population is grossly fat, and over one half of the residents suffer from diabetes, a disease that stems from dangerously high blood sugar.[19]

Realizing that they were poisoning themselves, some Pima returned to their traditional diet. When they ate native foods, both their obesity and high levels of blood sugar diminished. Other health problems, such as diabetes and heart disease, lessened as the pounds melted away. What is the magic of native foods?

At first, the doctors thought that a decrease in calories accounted for the weight loss. However, native foods proved to have more calories than they expected. Obviously, some other factor was at work. Now we know that it was the Good Calorie content of the diet.

GOOD CALORIES WORK ONLY ON THOSE WHO SUFFER FROM THE STARVATION RESPONSE

If Good Calories are such miracle workers, why have they remained unknown until now? To answer this question, you have to consider the nature of medicines. A headache tablet, for example, will do nothing for a person who does not have a headache. Similarly, Good Calories will do nothing for people who do not suffer from the Starvation Response. Replacing Bad Calories with Good Calories lowers blood sugar, insulin, and triglycerides in people who exhibit the Starvation Response, but does not have the same effect in 'normal' people (see Figures 7-1, 7-2 and 7-3 in Appendix 1).

To study the Starvation Response properly, you must remove all the Starvation Response triggers and use the entire programme on those who suffer from the Starvation Response.

ADDITIONAL BENEFITS OF THE GOOD CALORIE DIET

Weight loss is only one of the many benefits of the Good Calorie Diet. Here are just a few of the added health benefits:

Diabetes. The most common form of diabetes is adult-onset non-insulin-dependent diabetes melitus (NIDDM). When Australian doctors compared the effects of Good Calories versus the effects of the usual treatment of NIDDM, they found that Good Calories produced lower blood sugar and less urinary excretion of blood sugar.[23] Other doctors have confirmed the effectiveness of Good Calories in the treatment of NIDDM and insulin-dependent diabetes.[24] Good Calories also help prevent the fat from binding to the protein in muscle – the primary cause of diabetic complications.[25]

Note: Persons with diabetes should not change their diets without consulting their doctor.

Hypoglycaemia. Hypoglycaemia is a disease of low blood sugar. Its symptoms include headache, fatigue, irritability, anxiety, confusion, sweating and poor concentration. It usually occurs after eating Bad Calories and is characterized by initial increases in blood sugar followed by rapid decreases to lower-than-normal levels.

Good Calories are often an effective treatment for hypoglycaemia. They promote the gradual increase in blood sugar that does not trigger the rapid release of insulin that produces low blood sugar.

Heart disease. A 15-year study of 7,038 French policemen found that the earliest marker of heart disease is elevated insulin, a symptom of the Starvation Response.[26] The Starvation Response also raises levels of triglycerides, cholesterol and fatty acids, all of which contribute to heart disease.

Numerous studies have shown that Good Calories can lower, by nearly 30 per cent, the low-density lipoproteins (LDLs) in people who experience the Starvation Response; high levels of LDLs are correlated with heart attacks.[27] Only three weeks of adding four ounces of beans – the best Good Calories – per day to a normal diet lowers cholesterol by more than 10 per cent.[28]

Ageing. Only one thing has been shown to extend

the life span of mammals significantly, and that is caloric restriction. Animals that are fed low-calorie, nutritionally complete meals from birth live up to 60 per cent longer. If caloric restriction is delayed until adulthood, animals experience only a 20 per cent extension of the life span. The Good Calorie Diet may be an easy way to have the advantages of caloric restriction without eating less.

Cancer. One-third to one-half of all cancers may have a dietary origin.[29] Certainly, many researchers have noted a correlation between cancer and the ingestion of animal fats. Good Calories are known to help prevent prostate and colon cancer.[30]

Dental Caries (cavities). Dental caries are caused when Bad Calories, which are easily digested, release sugar into the mouth. Therefore, Good Calorie foods may help prevent them.[31]

Endurance and Fatigue. An additional advantage of Good Calories is that they foster endurance and lessen fatigue. Eating Good Calories (such as lentils) before exercise produces an 18 per cent increase in endurance, whereas exercise drinks produce only a 9 per cent increase.[32] Thus, a Good Calorie diet may be more than twice as effective as are many common exercise drinks in increasing endurance.

Part 2

Introduction

Part 2 was designed to make it easy to implement the Good Calorie Diet. The chapters address some questions that were unanswered by Part 1. They should offer the examples and guidance needed to make implementing my programme as painless as possible.

Chapter 8 offers a list of suggested menus for the two stages of the Good Calorie Diet: vegetarian menus for combating the Starvation Response and a programme for introducing animal products during the weight loss and maintenance portions of the diet. Many menu items are preceded by an asterix, indicating that the recipes for those items are presented in Chapter 9. These menus are included only to help show you the great diversity of foods and meals available to you. Feel free to substitute comparable foods. The only guidelines that must be followed closely are those concerning the timing of meals containing animal products, given in a short section immediately preceding the sample menus.

Chapter 10 surveys many restaurant menus and indicates which items are your best bets. Unlike the other chapters, this one is not strictly divided into Good and Bad Calories because of the immense variations in cooking styles among chefs. Instead, it highlights the items that are least likely to be harmful. You can also use Chapter 10 to get ideas for dishes that you may want to include in menus at home.

Chapter 11 is the most technical and, for most people, will be the least used. It lists the glycaemic indexes of foods that have actually been measured. Most people do not need to know the glycaemic indexes of the foods they eat. It is sufficient to know if they are Good or Bad Calories, information that is presented in Chapter 12.

8

Sample Daily Menus

Please remember that the Good Calorie Diet offers a great deal of freedom. I have included these menus only as examples. I'm sure you will find that substituting many of your own low-fat recipes will work as well. Also, you should feel free to combine items from different parts of the menus. Just be sure to follow the Golden Dozen rules and avoid the Starvation Response triggers.

The suggested menus offer vegetarian options as well as ones that contain sources of animal protein. Remember that animal fat and protein can induce the Starvation Response. Therefore, you must be careful about eating them. When you re-introduce them into your diet after you have overcome the Starvation Response, they count as Bad Calories. Only later – about a month after your body is accustomed to digesting animal fat and protein – do they count as Good Calories. At that time, you can start to experiment with Bad Calorie meals. However, most people find that they can tolerate animal fat and protein only every other day without re-evoking the Starvation Response.

The following summarizes the maximum pace at which you can introduce animal fat and protein into your diet after conquering the Starvation Response.

You should test yourself after 10 and 14 days to see if the symptoms of the Starvation Response have subsided. You may notice that the symptoms subside after three or four days, though such encouraging signs do not indicate that they have decreased as much as possible. Only when the symptoms have reached their maximum state of decrease should you consider moving to Day 1 of the menus for introducing animal fat and protein. Remember that it is better to stay on a diet that is free of animal fat and protein for a few extra days than to eat these products before you have fully overcome the Starvation Response.

CONTENTS OF MENUS FOR REINTRODUCING ANIMAL FAT AND PROTEIN

The *only* time you can eat animal fat and protein without cheating is at lunch. All other meals should be similar to those that are eaten while overcoming the Starvation Response.

Day 1	Lunch: animal protein, but no starch or high glycaemic-index carbohydrates.
Days 2 and 3	No animal protein in any meal.
Day 4	Lunch: animal protein, but no starch or high glycaemic-index carbohydrates.
Days 5 and 6	No animal protein in any meal.
Day 7	Lunch: animal protein, but no starch or high glycaemic-index carbohydrates.

Days 8 and 9	No animal protein in any meal.
Day 10	Lunch: animal protein, but no starch or high glycaemic-index carbohydrates.
Days 11 and 12	No animal protein in any meal.
Day 13	Lunch: animal protein, but no starch or high glycaemic-index carbohydrates.
Day 14	No animal protein in any meal.
Day 15	Lunch: animal protein, but no starch or high glycaemic-index carbohydrates.
Day 16 and onward	Alternate the plans for Day 14 and Day 15.

After two months without symptoms of the Starvation Response, animal protein meals eaten every other day are no longer considered to be Bad Calorie meals. At that point you can experiment with adding Bad Calorie meals according to the principles of Rules 11 and 12 of the Golden Dozen.

MENUS FOR USE BOTH WHILE CURING THE STARVATION RESPONSE AND ON VEGETARIAN DAYS DURING WEIGHT LOSS

I recommend a diet of Good Calories that excludes animal fats and protein while you are overcoming the Starvation Response and therefore this section contains only vegetarian meals.

* An asterisk before a recipe means that it is included in Chapter 9.

VEGETARIAN MENU 1

Breakfast: high fibre bran cereal with low-fat milk
orange juice
low-fat unsweetened yogurt

Lunch: *pasta with lemon and ginger
fresh vegetable crudities with *dill-yogurt
dip

Snack: low-fat bean dip, salsa and vegetable
crudities

Dinner: *vegetable medley soup
pasta with garlic, olive oil and broccoli
fruit smoothie drink of frozen fruits
blended with low-fat plain yogurt

VEGETARIAN MENU 2

Breakfast: old fashioned slow-cooked oatmeal
grapefruit

Lunch: *lentil stew with garlic and ginger
rice
fruit salad

Snack: cooked rice topped with berries and
flavoured low-fat unsweetened yogurt

Dinner: *spinach and garlic soup
baked vegetarian lasagne (seasoned and
layered aubergine pasta, courgettes,
low-fat cheese and tomato sauce)
grapes

VEGETARIAN MENU 3

Breakfast: sliced bananas and low-fat plain yogurt
high fibre bran cereal with low-fat milk
orange slices

Lunch: tossed green salad with low-fat salad
dressing
pasta sautéed in olive oil with sun-dried
tomatoes
melon with strawberries

Snack: pumpernickel sandwich with low-fat
cheese, low-fat mayonnaise, sliced
tomato and lettuce

Dinner: *gazpacho
*three-bean salad
low-fat cottage cheese
melon
slice whole-kernel rye bread

VEGETARIAN MENU 4

Breakfast: fresh fruit salad with low-fat plain yogurt
melon
old-fashioned slow-cooked oatmeal

Lunch: vegetarian chilli
garden salad with low-fat herb dressing
*pinto-bean dip with vegetable sticks

Snack: low-fat cottage cheese with assorted
vegetable sticks

Dinner: *Cuban black bean soup
rice with salsa
sponge cake

VEGETARIAN MENU 5

Breakfast: grapefruit
            low-fat cottage-cheese crêpes with low-fat
                yogurt and fresh fruit topping
Lunch: *Indian dhal (lentil) soup
            *baked tomatoes
            *saffron rice
            100 per cent rye bread
Snack: slice of vegetable pizza with a moderate
                amount of cheese
Dinner: *miso-soup with spring onions and
                seaweed
            *cucumber salad with vinegar-herb
                dressing
            pumpernickel toast with corn oil
                margarine
            *sugar-free strawberry jam

VEGETARIAN MENU 6

Breakfast: high fibre bran cereal with low-fat milk
            fruit
Lunch: *Russian borscht with low-fat yogurt
            pasta with pesto
            green salad with low-fat dressing
Snack: cheese sandwich on toasted rye bread
Dinner: *miso soup with spring onions and
                seaweed
            *three-bean salad
            *roasted vegetables

VEGETARIAN MENU 7

Breakfast: fresh citrus slices
               slice of dark pumpernickel bread
               unsaturated-fat margarine and
                   unsweetened jam
               low-fat cottage cheese
Lunch: *tomato-herb soup
               sautéed spring onions and vegetables
Snack: rice mixed with pesto
Dinner: mashed fresh tropical-fruit soup (chilled)
               *Good Calorie vegetable medley
               steamed rice
               sponge cake

VEGETARIAN MENU 8

Breakfast: stewed fresh fruit medley with low-fat
                   yogurt
Lunch: cold lentil salad on spinach
               pasta with low-fat marinara sauce
               apple slices
Snack: low-fat cheese toasted sandwich 100 per
                 cent rye bread
Dinner: tomato juice
               *white beans and garlic purée
               broccoli with toasted sesame seeds and
                   unsaturated margarine
               pumpernickel bread with unsweetened
                   jam
               sponge cake with banana (not overly ripe)
                 and strawberries

VEGETARIAN MENU 9

Breakfast: old-fashioned slow-cooked oatmeal with
                 heated fresh fruit
            melon
Lunch: gazpacho
            *linguine with shiitake mushroom sauce
            fresh seasonal fruit
Snack: rye toast with *sugar-free jam
Dinner: cold asparagus with low-fat yogurt and
                 curry sauce
            lentil soup
            herb-flavoured rice
            mixture of star fruit, papaya, strawberries
                 and raspberries

VEGETARIAN MENU 10

Breakfast: rice topped with *sugar-free strawberry
            jam
            orange juice
Lunch: grilled halibut with low-fat tomato sauce
            steamed vegetables with chutney
            *fruit ice or 'granita'
Snack: melon
Dinner: *Middle Eastern chickpea-cabbage soup
            *stewed tomatoes and okra
            baked yams
            *cranberry-ginger-orange relish

VEGETARIAN MENU 11

Breakfast: high fibre bran cereal with low-fat milk
          grapefruit
Lunch: *Indian dhal (lentil) soup
       rice
       grilled vegetable kebabs (green peppers,
          tomato, yam, orange, celery and
          cabbage) marinated in low-fat Italian
          dressing
       fresh strawberries
Snack: low-fat mild black-bean dip on rye bread
Dinner: low-fat coleslaw
       *horseradish and beetroot purée
       *purée of butternut squash

VEGETARIAN MENU 12

Breakfast: old-fashioned slow-cooked oatmeal
          orange slices
Lunch: *lentil-stuffed courgettes
       rice with herbs
       melon
Snack: unsweetened frozen fruit bars
Dinner: *cucumber salad with vinegar-herb
          dressing
       vegetarian chilli
       pumpernickel toast
       fruit

VEGETARIAN MENU 13

Breakfast: old-fashioned slow-cooked oatmeal with
          low-fat milk
          fruit

Lunch: linguine with *yellow bell-pepper sauce
           tropical fruit salad
Snack: fresh apple slices and low-fat cheese
Dinner: brown rice, lima beans and steamed
               vegetables with balsamic vinegar
           green salad
           wheat-free and sugar-free cookies

VEGETARIAN MENU 14

Breakfast: slow-cooked oatmeal with low-fat milk
           orange juice
           pumpernickel toast
           *sugar-free strawberry jam
Lunch: spinach salad with mushrooms and low-
               fat dressing
           low-fat pizza
Snack: fresh vegetable crudities (cucumber, celery
               and so on) with *dill-yogurt dip
Dinner: *three-bean salad
           steamed cauliflower and spinach with
               seasonings
           herbed rice

VEGETARIAN MENU 15

Breakfast: cooked, cooled rice topped with *sugar-
               free strawberry jam
           orange juice
Lunch: mixed beans, arugula and radicchio with
               balsamic vinaigrette
           *pasta primavera
Snack: *cottage cheese toasts

Dinner: *basmati rice and split peas
fruit salad

VEGETARIAN MENU 16

Breakfast: old-fashioned slow-cooked oatmeal with
low-fat milk
orange juice
pumpernickel toast
sugar-free jam
Lunch: *gazpacho
*lentil stew with garlic and ginger
rice
fruit salad
Snack: cooked, cooled rice topped with berries
and flavoured low-fat yogurt
Dinner: *savoury baked yams
baked vegetarian lasagne (seasoned and
layered aubergine pasta, courgettes, low
fat cheese and tomato sauce)
grapes

VEGETARIAN MENU 17

Breakfast: old-fashioned slow-cooked oatmeal
melon
juice
Lunch: *spring asparagus soup
*black-eyed pea salad
steamed or *roasted vegetables
Snack: grilled open-face pumpernickel sandwich
with low-fat cottage cheese, green
onion, sweet basil and a thin slice of
low-fat cheese

Dinner: *cucumber salad with vinegar-herb
                 dressing
             *fresh broccoli with lemon vinaigrette
             *bean and pumpkin stew

VEGETARIAN MENU 18

Breakfast: flavoured low-fat yogurt
             old-fashioned slow-cooked oatmeal with
                 fresh fruit cooked in the cereal
Lunch: tomato and onion salad with low-fat
                 dressing
             pasta with steamed vegetables and pesto
             *fruit ice
Snack: *Russian borscht with a small amount of
                 low-fat sour cream and/or cucumber
Dinner: green salad with low-fat dressing
             *white beans and garlic purée
             rye toast
             sponge cake with partially thawed frozen
                 berry topping

VEGETARIAN MENU 19

Breakfast: sliced bananas (not overly ripe) and low-
                 fat plain yogurt
             high fibre bran cereal with low-fat milk
             toasted whole-kernel bread with low-fat
                 unsaturated oil margarine
Lunch: *Russian borscht
             *chickpea flour quiche
             *wild rice salad
             papaya

Snack: cold tomato and basil soup garnished
               with low-fat yogurt
Dinner: *red and green salad with oriental
               dressing
            pasta with olive oil and garlic

MENUS CONTAINING ANIMAL PRODUCTS, TO BE INTRODUCED SLOWLY AFTER CURING THE STARVATION RESPONSE

This section features some lunches with animal products and contains vegetarian menus in all dinners and some lunches.

* An asterisk before a recipe means that it is included in Chapter 9.

MENU A

Breakfast: old-fashioned slow-cooked oatmeal
               melon
               juice
Lunch: prawn cocktail with *horseradish dip
            *Turkish cucumber-yogurt soup
            *salmon and black bean sauce
Snack: fruit shakes made from fruit, low-fat
               yogurt and ice, blended
Dinner: white bean soup
            *aubergine-tomato stew
            rice

MENU B

Breakfast: old-fashioned slow-cooked oatmeal
          orange slices
          whole-kernel bread, toasted
Lunch: vegetable soup with kidney beans
          rye bread
          *Mexican chicken fajitas
          honeydew melon
Snack: lean ham rolled around low-fat cheese
Dinner: *creamy winter squash soup
          pasta with low-fat marinara sauce

MENU C

Breakfast: fruit compote
          high fibre bran cereal with low-fat milk
Lunch: *red and green salad with oriental
             dressing
          *grilled sea bass with dill sauce
          fresh apple and grapes
Snack: *gazpacho
Dinner: *cantaloupe soup
          *pasta fagioli
          spinach with sesame

MENU D

Breakfast: low-fat cottage cheese crêpes with low-fat
          yogurt and fresh fruit topping
          lean ham
          grapefruit juice

Lunch: *Cuban black bean soup
           *New Orleans fettucine with mussels
           *Fruit ice or 'granita'
Snack: citrus fruit salad
Dinner: aubergine-tomato stew
           *pinto bean dip on pumpernickel toast
           *savoury baked yams

MENU E

Breakfast: papaya
           baked yams with unsaturated fat
              margarine
Lunch: grilled trout with *yellow bell-pepper
              sauce
           steamed green beans
           curried unsweetened apple sauce
           fresh fruit
Snack: cold cooked rice with cinnamon and diced
              fruit covered with low-fat milk
Dinner: *Middle Eastern chickpea-cabbage soup
           *stewed tomatoes and okra
           unsweetened frozen fruit bars

MENU F

Breakfast: high fibre bran cereal with low-fat milk
           orange juice
           low-fat plain yogurt
Lunch: split-pea soup
           *Good Calorie chicken salad
           baked butternut squash
           cantaloupe with berries and banana

Snack: low-fat cheese toasted sandwich 100 per
           cent rye bread
Dinner: *Indian dhal (lentil) soup
           rice
           grilled yams
           fresh strawberries

MENU G

Breakfast: fresh citrus slices
           slice of dark pumpernickel bread
           unsaturated-fat margarine and
               unsweetened jam
           low-fat cottage cheese
Lunch: Japanese-style clear miso broth with
               spinach and cabbage
           *chicken and beetroot salad
           sliced orange and apple
Snack: low-fat bean dip, salsa and low-fat tortilla
               chips
Dinner: *spinach and garlic soup
           grilled vegetable kebabs (green peppers,
               tomato, yam, orange, celery and
               cabbage), marinated in low-fat Italian
               dressing
           grapefruit ice

MENU H

Breakfast: old-fashioned slow-cooked oatmeal
           low-fat plain yogurt over fresh fruit slices
Lunch: *Turkish cucumber-yogurt soup
           mixed baby greens with balsamic vinegar
               and olive oil
           *marinated chicken breasts

Snack: mild black-bean dip spread on rye bread
Dinner: sautéed mushrooms and broccoli on rice
          *purée of butternut squash

MENU I

Breakfast: sliced bananas (not overly ripe) and low-
           fat plain yogurt
           old-fashioned slow-cooked oatmeal with
             low-fat milk
           toasted whole-kernel bread with low-fat
             unsaturated oil or margarine
Lunch: *grilled halibut with green sauce
           *savoury baked yams
Snack: low-fat cheese on whole-kernel bread
Dinner: mashed fresh tropical-fruit soup (chilled)
           stir-fried vegetables and rice
           sponge cake

MENU J

Breakfast: cooked white rice with sugar-free jam
           fruit
           melted low-fat cheese on 100 per cent rye
             toast
Lunch: *cantaloupe soup
           *spicy chicken salad
           steamed broccoli with cauliflower
Snack: fruit
Dinner: *marinated green tomato salad
           *pasta fagioli

MENU K

Breakfast: stewed fresh fruit
high fibre bran cereal with low-fat milk
Lunch: *prawns with lemon and ginger
steamed rice
brussels sprouts with light olive oil and
lemon
Snack: fruit
Dinner: *cucumber salad with vinegar-herb
dressing
*winter vegetable purée
*fruit ice or 'granita'

MENU L

Breakfast: sliced bananas and low-fat plain yogurt
high fibre bran cereal with low-fat milk
toasted whole-kernel bread with low-fat
unsaturated oil or margarine
Lunch: *Turkish cucumber-yogurt soup
*flounder with lemon-mustard sauce
*baked tomatoes
Snack: vegetable crudities with *Tzatziki-Greek
cucumber-yogurt dip
Dinner: *vegetable medley soup
pasta and low-fat tomato marinara with
steamed vegetables

MENU M

Breakfast:	fresh citrus slices
	slice of dark pumpernickel bread with unsaturated-fat margarine and unsweetened jam
	low-fat cottage cheese
Lunch:	*creamy winter squash soup
	*prawns with tomatoes
Snack:	fresh vegetable crudities (cucumber, celery and so on) with *horseradish dip
Dinner:	*oriental sweet potato stew
	rice

MENU N

Breakfast:	fresh fruit salad with low-fat plain yogurt
	melon
Lunch:	*orange-glazed turkey breast
	*horseradish and beetroot purée
	*Good Calorie vegetable medley
Snack:	fresh apple slices and low-fat cheese
Dinner:	*rice pilaf
	*mung bean-tomato stew

MENU O

Breakfast:	grapefruit
	old-fashioned slow-cooked oatmeal with stewed fresh fruit
	low-fat cottage cheese
Lunch:	spinach salad with low-fat dressing
	lean flank steak marinated in Dijon mustard

	*roasted vegetables
	diet sorbet
Snack:	fruit shake made from fruit, low-fat
	yogurt and ice, blended
Dinner:	herbed spaghetti

MENU P

Breakfast:	melon
	old-fashioned slow-cooked oatmeal with berries
Lunch:	*tomato-herb soup
	*prawns with lemon and ginger
	*saffron rice
Snack:	unsweetened frozen fruit bars
Dinner:	*red bean pistou
	cucumber and onion salad with seasoned low-fat yogurt dressing

---

MENU Q

Breakfast:	rice with sugar-free jam
	grapefruit
Lunch:	*marinated chicken breasts
	steamed vegetables
	*fruit ice or 'granita'
Snack:	apple slices with low-fat cheese
Dinner:	green salad with low-fat dressing
	*wild rice salad
	sponge cake with strawberries

9

Recipes

The main purpose of these recipes is to demonstrate the wonderful diversity of vegetarian meals, though these recipes certainly do not cover all the foods you can eat. Just look at Chapter 12 for other choices.

I purposely did not choose recipes that are extremely low in fat. Such extraordinary measures are not necessary in the Good Calorie Diet. However, that does not mean that you should not eat such foods. They can be extremely useful in balancing a Bad Calorie food that is slightly high in fat served in the same meal.

When you use recipes from other books, you should make sure that they feature Good Calories in at least a four-to-one ratio with Bad Calories.

You should also make sure that your alternate recipes do not derive greater than 30 per cent of their calories from fat. To calculate the percentage of calories that are derived from fat, multiply the grams of fat in one portion by 9 and divide that figure by the total number of calories in the portion. If you do not know the total calories in a food, multiply the grams of carbohydrate or protein by 4 and then add the calories derived from fat.

SALADS

MARINATED GREEN TOMATO SALAD
Serves 6–8

5 medium green tomatoes,
  sliced
1¹/₂ tsp olive oil
salt and pepper
2 tbsp red wine vinegar
  or cider vinegar

1 large garlic clove, chopped
1 small red onion, thinly
  chopped
2 tbsp chopped fresh
  tarragon

Preheat the grill.

Brush the tomato slices with olive oil. Sprinkle with salt and pepper and grill for about 2 minutes on each side until lightly browned.

Place the tomatoes in a shallow dish and sprinkle with vinegar, garlic, onion and tarragon. Marinate at least 4 hours or overnight.

Serve cold.

THREE-BEAN SALAD

Serves 8–10

5oz/150g cooked green beans
7oz/200g cooked or canned
   kidney beans, rinsed
7oz/200g cooked or canned
   white or pinto beans, rinsed
2 tbsp olive oil

2 tbsp balsamic vinegar
2 shallots, chopped
2 tbsp coarse-grain mustard
salt and pepper to taste
4 tbsp chopped fresh dill

Combine the three types of beans in a large mixing bowl and set aside. Place the olive oil, vinegar, shallots, mustard, salt and pepper in a small saucepan and heat, whisking constantly, until very hot, but not boiling. Pour the hot mixture over the beans and toss to coat thoroughly. Stir in the dill.

Can be served at room temperature or chilled.

CUCUMBER SALAD WITH
VINEGAR-HERB DRESSING

Serves 4

Salad:
2 small cucumbers,
  thinly sliced
1 celery stalk, chopped

Dressing:
4 tbsp rice vinegar
1 garlic clove, crushed
1 tbsp chopped fresh dill
  or 1 tsp dried dill

In a blender or food processor, blend all the ingredients for
the dressing and pour over the salad. Chill.

RED AND GREEN SALAD WITH
ORIENTAL DRESSING

Serves 4

Salad:
1 green pepper, cut in strips
1 red pepper, cut in strips
12oz/375g spinach leaves
small head of radicchio

Dressing:
7 tbsp low-fat Italian
  dressing
1 tbsp chopped fresh ginger
1 tsp orange zest
1 tbsp chopped fresh
  coriander

Arrange the fresh vegetables attractively on a platter.

Blend all the ingredients for the dressing in a blender or
food processor and pour over the vegetables.

WILD RICE SALAD

Serves 4–5

1lb/500g cooked wild rice
1lb/500g fresh peas, boiled
   briefly
2 tbsp white wine vinegar
2 spring onions, chopped

1 tart green apple, peeled,
   cored and chopped
2 tbsp olive oil
salt and pepper to taste

Combine all the ingredients in a medium-size bowl and mix.
Serve with meat or fish.

BLACK-EYED BEAN SALAD

Serves 10

1lb/500g dried black-eyed
   beans, washed and sorted
1¾ pt/1L cold water
2 medium onions, chopped
3 garlic cloves, crushed
2 tbsp olive oil

1 tsp dried marjoram
2 tsp salt
pepper to taste
3 tbsp cider vinegar
6 tbsp chopped fresh
   parsley

Soak the beans for 2 hours in large saucepan. Drain and
cover with fresh water. Over medium heat, bring the beans
to the boil. Cover and cook for 1 hour. Drain the beans and
transfer to a large bowl.

Add the onions, garlic, olive oil, marjoram, salt, pepper and
vinegar. Mix well. Add parsley and stir.

Chill several hours or overnight.

SOUP

BASIC VEGETABLE STOCK FOR SOUPS
AND STEWS, NO. 1

2 pt/1.2L water
5oz/150g dried wild or
   Japanese mushrooms or
   3 tbsp miso
3 carrots, coarsely grained
3 tbsp chopped fresh parsley

1 tbsp dried marjoram
1 tbsp soy sauce
   (wheat-free)
salt and pepper to taste

Combine all the ingredients except the soy sauce, salt and pepper in a large saucepan or stockpot and bring to the boil.

Reduce the heat to low and simmer for 30 minutes. Add the soy sauce, salt and pepper. Simmer an additional 5 minutes.

Experiment with the spices and herbs. Fresh herbs always give a wonderful taste; however, if you are short on time, dried herbs and spices are fine. Adjust the seasonings to taste.

Check the seasonings. Cool and reserve.

BASIC VEGETABLE STOCK FOR SOUPS
AND STEWS, NO. 2

3¹/₂ pt/2L water
1 medium onion, peeled and
  diced
3 carrots, coarsely grated
2 celery stalks, halved
5oz/150g leeks, washed and
  coarsely chopped
1 tbsp soy sauce (wheat-free)

3 tbsp chopped fresh
  parsley
1 tbsp dried marjoram
¹/₂ tsp cayenne pepper
2 sprigs fresh thyme
1 bay leaf
salt and pepper to taste

Combine all the ingredients except the soy sauce, salt and pepper, in a large saucepan or stockpot and bring to the boil.

Reduce the heat to low and simmer for 30 minutes. Add the soy sauce, salt and pepper. Simmer an additional 5 minutes.

Experiment with the spices and herbs. Fresh herbs always give a wonderful taste; however, if you are short on time, dried herbs and spices are fine. Adjust seasonings to taste.

Check seasonings. Cool and reserve.

CUBAN BLACK BEAN SOUP

Serves 12

4 slices extra lean bacon
1 medium onion, chopped
4 cloves garlic, chopped
4 celery stalks, chopped
2 jalapeño chillis, seeded and diced
3 tbsp ground cumin

3 tbsp oregano
1lb/500g black beans, soaked overnight
7 pt/4L water
4fl oz/125ml fresh lime juice
salt and pepper to taste
low-fat yogurt for garnish

Cook the bacon in a large saucepan or stockpot until almost crisp. Remove and set aside. Chop.

Add the onion, garlic and celery to the pot and sauté, stirring for about 10 minutes. Stir in the jalapeño chillis and continue to cook for approximately 5 more minutes. Stir in the cumin and oregano.

Rinse and drain the black beans and add to the pot with the water. Simmer until the beans are very soft, about 2 to 2½ hours. Thin with more water if the soup becomes too thick.

Stir in the lime juice and the reserved bacon. Garnish with low-fat yogurt. Serve.

TOMATO-HERB SOUP

Serves 12

2 tbsp olive oil
4 medium leeks (tender green
   and white parts only),
   washed thoroughly and
   sliced
2 carrots (coarsely grated)
1 medium onion, chopped
2 garlic cloves, crushed
1 tsp lemon zest
1 tsp dried tarragon
1 tsp saffron

10 large ripe tomatoes,
   seeded and diced
28oz/800g can of Italian
   plum tomatoes
8fl oz/250ml fresh orange
   juice
3½ pt/2L vegetable
   stock
2oz/50g chopped fresh basil
low-fat Parmesan cheese,
   grated (optional)

In a nonstick frying pan, heat the olive oil and add the leeks, carrots, onion and garlic. Sauté until soft for about 15 minutes.

Add the sauté to a large saucepan or stockpot. Add the lemon zest, tarragon and saffron and cook, stirring, for 3 minutes.

Add the fresh and canned tomatoes, orange juice, and vegetable stock and stir to combine.

Simmer over low heat for 30 minutes.

Remove from the heat and cool.

Purée the soup in batches in a blender or food processor and return to the stockpot. Before serving, warm the soup and stir in the basil.

Sprinkle with Parmesan cheese if desired.

INDIAN DAHL (LENTIL) SOUP

Serves 12

8oz/250g channa dhal (yellow
    split peas, available in
    Indian or oriental food
    shops)
2 pt/1.2L water
3 garlic cloves, chopped
1 in/2.5cm fresh ginger,
    peeled and chopped

1 tbsp cumin
salt to taste
cayenne pepper to taste
    (about $1/8$ tsp)
$1/2$ tsp garam masala
    (available in Indian or
    oriental food shops)

Wash the dhal thoroughly in several changes of water, drain and pick over for any grit or particles.

Put the dhal and water in a large saucepan or stockpot and bring to the boil. Skim off any scum from the surface.

Add the turmeric, garlic, ginger and cumin; turn the heat to low; and cook, partially covered, for about 1½ hours, until the dhal is soft. Stir frequently to prevent sticking.

After the dhal is tender, add the salt, cayenne pepper, and garam masala. Stir and cook for an additional 15 minutes.

Serve with rice.

CREAMY WINTER SQUASH SOUP

Serves 12

2 tbsp olive oil
1lb/500g medium leeks
   (white and tender green
   only), washed thoroughly
   and sliced
3 garlic cloves, crushed
2lb/1000g butternut or acorn
   squash (about 3 large),
   peeled and cubed
2½ pt/1.5L
   vegetable stock

1 tbsp curry powder
1 tsp ground coriander
salt and pepper to taste
2 tbsp peeled fresh ginger,
   chopped
8oz/250g non-fat yogurt
3 tbsp fresh lime juice

In a frying pan, heat the olive oil and sauté the leeks and garlic until soft. Reserve.

In a large saucepan or stockpot, add the squash and the vegetable stock.

Bring to the boil; turn the heat to low and add the curry powder, coriander, salt and pepper. Simmer while adding the sautéed leeks, garlic and ginger and continue to simmer for about 45 minutes until the squash is very soft.

Let cool slightly.

Purée the soup in batches in a blender or food processor and return to the saucepan.

Adjust the seasonings. Stir in the yogurt and add lime juice to taste. Serve hot or cold.

MIDDLE EASTERN CHICKPEA AND CABBAGE SOUP

Serves 8

6oz/175g dried chickpeas,
  rinsed and cleaned
2½ pints/1.4L water
1 medium onion, chopped
1 large yam, peeled and
  cubed
1 small can tomatoes

1 small head of cabbage,
  finely chopped
1oz/25g chopped fresh dill
2 tsp tomato purée
salt and pepper to taste

Cover the chickpeas with water and soak for 12 hours or overnight. Drain and rinse.

Add the onion and chickpeas to a large saucepan or stockpot and cover with 2 pints of water. Bring to the boil. Turn the heat to low, cover partially and simmer for 1 hour.

Add the yam, tomato, cabbage, dill, tomato paste, salt, pepper and the remaining water. Cover, simmer for a further hour, adjust seasonings and serve.

RUSSIAN BORSCHT

Serves 6–8

1lb/500g beetroot, sliced and
  cooked
1 medium onion, chopped
2 carrots, coarsely grated
1 leek (white and tender
  green parts only), washed
  thoroughly and sliced
2 celery stalks, chopped
1 bay leaf

salt and pepper to taste
1 tbsp sherry or cider
  vinegar
3 1/2 pt/2L
  vegetable stock or water
lemon juice to taste (2–4
  tbsp)
8oz/250g plain low-fat
  yogurt

In a large stockpot, combine the beetroot, onions, carrots,
leek, celery, bay leaf, sherry or vinegar and vegetable stock
or water. Bring to the boil, reduce the heat to low and
simmer for 1 hour, or until the vegetables are very soft.

Strain all the vegetables and stock through a sieve and
discard the vegetables.

Stir in the lemon juice and serve either hot or cold, topped
with the low-fat yogurt.

CANTALOUPE SOUP

Serves 6–8

2 large ripe melons
4fl oz/125ml fresh orange
   juice
2 tbsp sweet white wine
1 tsp chopped fresh mint

1 teaspoon grated fresh
   ginger
4fl oz/125g low fat yogurt
fresh strawberries (optional)

Cut the melons in half and remove the seeds. Remove the skin from the melons and dice the fruit.

Purée the melons, orange juice, wine, mint and ginger in a blender or food processor.

Add the yogurt and blend.

Refrigerate and serve cold with fresh strawberries to garnish, if desired.

SPRING ASPARAGUS SOUP

Serves 6–8

Prepare the stock (can be
   done 1 day ahead and
   refrigerated):
1lb/500g tender young
   asparagus
12oz/375g leeks (tender
   green and white parts only),
   washed thoroughly
   and sliced

1 bay leaf
2 celery stalks, chopped
2¾ pt /1.6L water
salt and pepper to taste

Chop the asparagus into small pieces. Combine all the ingredients in a large stockpot and bring to the boil. Reduce the heat to low and simmer for 30 minutes. Strain, discard the solids, and reserve the broth. Prepare the soup:

3 leeks (white and tender green parts only), washed thoroughly and sliced	2.4pt/1.4L reserved stock
	salt and pepper to taste
	lemon juice (optional)
2 garlic cloves, crushed	4oz/125g low-fat plain
1lb/500g trimmed asparagus	yogurt
2 tbsp chopped fresh parsley	

Steam the leeks and garlic in a vegetable basket until tender.

Add the leeks and garlic, asparagus, parsley, stock, salt and pepper to a large stockpot.

Bring to the boil, reduce the heat to low, and simmer until the asparagus is tender, about 8-10 minutes. Cool slightly.

Purée the soup in a blender or food processor and then strain.

Return the strained mixture to the pot; season with lemon juice, if desired; and stir in the yogurt. Serve.

MISO SOUP WITH SPRING ONIONS AND SEAWEED

Serves 4

1³/₄pt/1L water
1 strip chopped *kombu*
   seaweed approximately
   10in x 3in/25cm x 7.5cm
   (available in oriental
   foodshops)
4 tbsp dark yellow miso

⅛ tsp 7-spice seasoning
   (available in oriental
   groceries)
chopped spring onions
1 tbsp Japanese chopped
   seaweed

Bring the water to the boil in a large saucepan or stockpot. Wipe the kombu with a damp cloth and immerse in the boiling water. Turn off the heat and steep the kombu for about 3 minutes. Remove the kombu. Add the miso and seasoning and boil for an additional 5 minutes. Strain the broth through a fine sieve.

Serve with a garnish of chopped spring onions and seaweed.

GAZPACHO

Serves 4

2 garlic cloves, chopped
2 tbsp lemon juice
5 large ripe tomatoes, coarsely chopped
1 bunch spring onions, finely chopped
1 cucumber, peeled and very thinly sliced
1 green pepper, seeded and finely chopped
1 yellow pepper, seeded and finely chopped
1 small can of vegetable/tomato juice
1 tbsp balsamic vinegar
salt and pepper to taste

In a blender or food processor, purée the garlic and lemon juice to a smooth paste. In a large bowl, add all the vegetables to the garlic paste; toss to combine; and stir in the vegetable/tomato juice, balsamic vinegar, salt and pepper.

Purée half the soup in a blender or food processor and recombine with the soup remaining in the bowl. Refrigerate until cold.

RED BEAN PISTOU

Serves 6–8

Soup:
3 tbsp olive oil
1 large onion, chopped
3 garlic cloves, crushed
2 tbsp oregano
1 tbsp thyme
1 large can (28oz/800g)
   Italian tomatoes
1³/₄pt/1L vegetable stock
1 tsp paprika
1 tsp celery salt
1 tsp mustard powder
salt and pepper to taste
2 small courgettes, diced
2oz/50g rice
3 cups red kidney beans,
   cooked

Basil gremolata:
4 tbsp fresh parsley leaves
4oz/125g fresh basil leaves
1 large garlic clove, crushed
1 tbsp olive oil
1 tbsp low-fat Parmesan
   cheese

Prepare the soup:

In a large saucepan or stockpot, heat the olive oil over a low heat. Add the onion, garlic, oregano and thyme. Cook for about 10 minutes until the onion is soft.

Add the tomatoes, stock, and seasoning. Salt and pepper to taste.

Bring to the boil, reduce the heat to low, and simmer for 25 minutes.

Add the courgettes, rice and cooked beans. Simmer for an additional 20 minutes.

Prepare the gremolata:

Combine the parsley, basil and garlic in a blender or food processor and process until finely minced. Add the olive oil and process to a paste. Add the Parmesan cheese and blend. Reserve.

Serve the soup hot with a dollop of gremolata.

TURKISH CUCUMBER-YOGURT SOUP

Serves 4

1lb/500g plain low-fat
   yogurt
4fl oz/125ml skimmed milk
1 medium cucumber, peeled,
   seeded and diced
salt and pepper to taste

2 garlic cloves, crushed
1 tbsp olive oil
1 tbsp fresh dill, chopped

In a bowl, whisk together the yogurt and milk until smooth. Add the cucumbers, salt, pepper, garlic and oil and mix well. Serve chilled, garnished with dill.

SPINACH AND GARLIC SOUP

Serves 6–8

3¹/₂ pt/2L vegetable stock
   or water
2 tsp olive oil
6 large garlic cloves, sliced
1 medium onion, chopped

1 carrot, grated
2 celery stalks, chopped
6oz/175g stale rye bread
   crumbs
3 cups spinach, finely
   chopped
salt and pepper to taste

Place the vegetable stock or water in a large stockpot and
bring to a simmer. Add the olive oil, garlic, onion, carrots
and celery. Simmer for approximately 25 minutes, until the
vegetables are soft. Add the bread crumbs.

Remove from the heat and cool slightly. Purée the soup in a
blender or food processor and return to the pot. Bring to a
simmer and add the spinach. Heat thoroughly to blend the
flavours.

VEGETABLE MEDLEY SOUP

Serves 8

2 tbsp olive oil

1 large onion, chopped

4 garlic cloves, crushed

7 pt/4L vegetable stock

4 carrots, chopped

4 celery stalks, chopped

2 tbsp dried rosemary

2 tsp paprika

2 tsp celery salt

2 tsp mustard powder

2 tbsp dried basil

salt and pepper to taste

2 yams, peeled and cubed

7oz/200g can of lima beans

   or butter beans

1 head of escarole

1 x 28-oz can Italian

   tomatoes

In a frying pan, heat the olive oil and sauté the onion and garlic until soft. Add the sautéed vegetables, vegetable stock, carrots, celery, and seasonings to a large stockpot and bring to the boil. Reduce the heat to a simmer, add the yams, and continue to cook for about 45 minutes, until the yams are soft. Add the lima beans, escarole, and tomatoes and cook for an additional 20 minutes. Adjust the seasonings and serve.

VEGETARIAN MAIN DISHES

MUNG BEAN AND TOMATO STEW

Serves 8

6oz/175g whole mung beans
2 pt/1.2L water
3 tbsp olive oil
8 garlic cloves, crushed

1 large onion, chopped
1x28oz/800g can tomatoes
1/2lb/250g spinach,
    cleaned and chopped
salt and pepper
2 tbsp fresh lime juice

Clean and pick over the mung beans. Wash thoroughly in several changes of water. Drain. Put the beans and water in a large saucepan or stockpot and bring to the boil. Turn the heat to low.

Cover and simmer for 3 minutes.

Turn off the heat and allow to rest, covered, for 1 hour.

Bring to the boil, reduce the heat to low and simmer for an additional 1 1/2 hours until the beans are slightly mushy. Stir to avoid sticking. Drain the beans and reserve. Reserve water to add to sauce if thinning is needed.

Heat the olive oil in a large saucepan and add the garlic. Stir-fry the garlic until it is slightly browned. Add the onion and sauté until translucent.

Add the tomatoes and stir-fry for 4-5 minutes. Add the

beans and bring to a simmer. Cook for 5 minutes.

Add the spinach, salt and pepper and lime juice and simmer for an additional 5 minutes until the spinach is cooked.

Serve with rice and lime wedges, if desired.

ORIENTAL SWEET POTATO STEW

Serves 6

2 tbsp olive oil
3 garlic cloves, crushed
2 tbsp fresh ginger
   peeled and minced
1lb/500g sweet potatoes,
   peeled and cubed
1/2lb/250g fresh green
   beans, trimmed and cut
   in 1/2 in/1cm lengths

2 carrots, peeled and cut in
   1/2 in/1cm slices
6oz/175g mushrooms
3/4 pt/450ml water
4 tbsp soy sauce
1 tbsp sherry (optional,
   alcohol will cook away)

Heat the olive oil in a heavy frying pan over medium heat. Add the garlic and ginger and stir-fry for 1 minute. Using a slotted spoon, transfer the vegetables, not the oil, to a large, heavy saucepan.

Add the sweet potatoes, green beans, and carrots and stir-fry for 1 minute.

Add the mushrooms and stir-fry for another minute.

Add the water, soy sauce and sherry.

Cover and simmer over a low heat for about 25-30 minutes until the sweet potatoes are tender. Remove the cover, raise the heat to high, and boil until the sauce is reduced and slightly thickened. Stir gently.

Serve with rice, if desired, or as a side dish.

AUBERGINE AND TOMATO STEW

Serves 6

1 large aubergine, peeled
   and cubed
3 garlic cloves, minced
1 in/2.5cm fresh ginger,
   peeled and chopped
3 large tomatoes, chopped
3/4oz/20g fresh parsley

7oz/200g cooked lima
   beans or butter beans
2 tbsp soy sauce (wheat-
   free)
salt and pepper to taste
4 tbsp olive oil
1 bunch spring onions,
   chopped

Preheat the oven to 180°C/350°F/Gas Mark 4. Bake the aubergine cubes for about 25 minutes until almost tender.

Meanwhile, heat the olive oil in a small saucepan and sauté the garlic and ginger, stirring for about 7-8 minutes until soft. Do not brown. Remove the vegetables and transfer them to a large saucepan.

Add the tomatoes, parsley, lima beans, soy sauce, salt and pepper to the saucepan and simmer on a low heat for 20 minutes, stirring and mashing the tomatoes with the back of a wooden spoon.

Add the reserved aubergine to the saucepan and continue to cook until soft.

Adjust the seasonings and garnish with spring onions.

LENTIL STEW WITH GARLIC AND GINGER

Serves 8–10

8oz/250g dry lentils, rinsed
1 tbsp curry powder
2 tbsp turmeric
1 tsp paprika
1 tsp celery salt
1 tsp mustard powder
1 tsp coriander
1 tsp ground cumin
1 tsp dried basil

salt and pepper to taste
7 pt/4L water
2 celery stalks, chopped
2 large yams, peeled and
    cubed
1/2 in/1cm piece of fresh
    ginger, peeled and
    chopped
5 large garlic cloves,
    chopped
3 tbsp tomato paste

In a large saucepan, cover the lentils with the water and bring to the boil. Stir in all the dry seasonings, turn the heat to low, and simmer for 30 minutes. Add the vegetables, ginger, garlic, and tomato paste and cook until the yams are tender. Adjust the seasonings and serve.

BEAN AND PUMPKIN STEW

Serves 6–8

7oz/200g white or pinto
   beans
1 medium onion, chopped
3 garlic cloves, minced
2 tbsp olive oil
14oz/400g can of tomatoes
1 tsp ground cinnamon
1 tbsp ground cumin

2 whole cloves (do not eat!)
1 tbsp Hungarian-style
   hot paprika
3/4–11/4pt/450-750ml
   vegetable broth
1 small pumpkin, peeled,
   seeded, and diced
salt and pepper to taste

Soak the beans for 6 hours or overnight. Drain and rinse.
Reserve.

In large, heavy saucepan, sauté the onions and garlic in the
olive oil for about 5–6 minutes, until soft. Do not brown.

Add the tomatoes, cinnamon, cumin, cloves, paprika and 1
cup of the vegetable broth. Simmer for 10 minutes, then add
the remaining broth, beans, pumpkin, salt and pepper.

Cook on low heat for about 1–1 1/2 hours, until the pumpkin
is very tender.

Adjust the seasonings; add additional salt if necessary.

LINGUINE WITH SHIITAKE MUSHROOM SAUCE

Serves 4

1oz/25g dried shiitake
   mushrooms
8 fl oz/250ml boiling water
3 tbsp olive oil
4 shallots, finely chopped
5oz/150g fresh mushrooms,
   sliced

1/2 tsp dried rosemary
1 cup low-fat yogurt
1lb/500g dried linguine
8fl oz/250ml vegetable
   stock

Soak the dried mushrooms in hot water for about 30 minutes until soft.

Drain and squeeze out the excess water. Discard the stems and reserve the mushrooms and liquid separately.

Heat the olive oil in a saucepan and sauté the shallots until tender. Add the dried reserved mushrooms, fresh mushrooms and rosemary.

Add the vegetable stock and the reserved mushroom liquid.

Boil for about 10 minutes until reduced to a thick glaze.

Add the yogurt and blend.

Cook the linguine. Serve with the sauce.

WINTER VEGETABLE PURÉE

Serves 8–10

	Bouquet garni:
2 yams	3 thyme sprigs
3lb/1.25kg celeriac	1 bay leaf
10 medium turnips	2 garlic cloves
3 garlic cloves	6 parsley sprigs
4 medium leeks	10 black peppercorns
salt and pepper to taste	
8oz/250g low-fat yogurt	

Peel the yams, celeriac, turnips and garlic. Trim the leeks and wash well. Chop the vegetables coarsely and make a bouquet garni by encasing the herbs in a piece of butter muslin.

Place all the vegetables in a large saucepan with barely enough water to cover them and the bouquet garni. Simmer, covered, for about 20 minutes, or until the vegetables are tender.

Remove the bouquet garni, drain the vegetables, and purée them in a blender or food processor, adding the yogurt, until smooth.

Add salt and pepper to taste.

Keep warm in a double boiler and serve.

CHICKPEA FLOUR QUICHE

Serves 6–8

10oz/300g chickpea flour, sifted

2 pt/1.2L water

4 garlic cloves, chopped

1/2 tsp grated ginger

1 tsp ground cumin

1/2 tsp turmeric

1/8 to 1/4 tsp cayenne pepper (to taste)

1 tbsp fresh parsley, chopped

3 tbsp olive oil

1 medium onion, sliced

1 tbsp lemon juice

2 tsp salt

red and yellow pepper slices, for garnish

In a large mixing bowl, slowly add the water to the chickpea flour, smoothing out any lumps. Set aside.

Add the garlic, ginger, parsley, cumin, turmeric, cayenne, and parsley to 1/3 pint of additional water; mix and set aside.

Heat the olive oil in a large saucepan, add the onion, and stir-fry for 3–4 minutes.

Add the spices and stir-fry for 1 more minute.

Add the chickpea mixture and bring to the boil, stirring constantly.

Turn the heat to medium low and continue stirring for about 15 minutes until the mixture begins to leave the sides of the saucepan.

Add the lemon juice and salt. Taste.

Empty the mixture into a 9in/23cm cake tin and allow to cool to room temperature.

Add slices of red and yellow peppers to garnish.

LENTIL-STUFFED COURGETTES

Serves 8

4 medium courgettes
  (about 2lb) scrubbed with
  ends trimmed
2 tbsp olive oil
1 medium onion, chopped
3 garlic cloves, crushed

1 tsp cumin
salt and pepper to taste
6oz/150g cooked lentils
6oz/150g cooked rice
low-fat Parmesan cheese

Cut the courgettes in half and scoop out the centres. Steam, covered, for 8 minutes.

Heat the olive oil in a frying pan and add the onion and garlic. Sauté until soft.

Add the cumin, salt and pepper. Stir-fry for 1 minute.

Combine the lentils and rice. Mix the onion mixture into the combined lentils and rice and stuff the courgette with the mixture. Sprinkle with Parmesan cheese and place under the grill until lightly browned. Serve hot.

ROASTED VEGETABLES

Serves 6

This method is a wonderful way to serve fresh asparagus and can be used with aubergines, peppers, broccoli, and cauliflower as well. The roasting time for the vegetables varies, broccoli and cauliflower taking the longest. Check the tenderness of the vegetables during cooking.

1lb/500g fresh asparagus, trimmed	1 tbsp dried rosemary
2 tbsp coarse salt	olive oil

Preheat the oven to 190°C/375°F/Gas Mark 5. Arrange the asparagus in a single layer in a large baking tin. Sprinkle the salt and rosemary over the asparagus and drizzle sparingly with olive oil. Roast for about 6–7 minutes until crisp-tender.

PASTA PRIMAVERA

Serves 4

1lb/500g cooked linguine	1 small bunch broccoli,
2 tbsp olive oil	cut into florets
2 garlic cloves, minced	salt and pepper to taste
1 medium red onion, sliced	low-fat Parmesan cheese
2 carrots, coarsely grated	

In a large frying pan heat the olive oil, add the garlic, and sauté until soft. Add the onion, separating the slices, and sauté for an additional 3 minutes. Add the carrots and broccoli.

Cover and steam, stirring occasionally, until the vegetables are crisp-tender. Add salt and pepper to taste. Simultaneously cook the pasta.

Toss the vegetable mixture with the cooked pasta and sprinkle with Parmesan cheese. Serve immediately.

PASTA FAGIOLI

Serves 8–10

14 oz/400g dried white
   beans, soaked overnight
   in water
2 tbsp olive oil
1 medium onion, chopped
2x14oz/400g can of crushed
   Italian plum tomatoes
3oz/75g pastina

1 tsp celery salt
1 tsp mustard powder
1 tbsp paprika
1 tbsp oregano
salt and pepper to taste
low fat Parmesan cheese
3 garlic cloves, chopped

Drain and rinse the beans. Place them in a large saucepan, cover with fresh water, and bring to the boil. Reduce the heat and simmer for about 1½ hours until very soft. Meanwhile, heat the olive oil in a skillet, sauté the onion and garlic for 8–10 minutes, and reserve.

Drain the beans, reserving the cooking liquid. Purée the beans in a blender, or food processor, adding small amounts of liquid, if needed. Return to the pot. Add the tomatoes, 1¾ pt/1L of cooking liquid, pastina, seasonings, salt and pepper.

Over low heat, cook for about 30 minutes until the pasta is tender. Sprinkle with Parmesan cheese, if desired.

NON VEGETARIAN MAIN DISHES

CHICKEN AND BEETROOT SALAD

Serves 2

1 tbsp Dijon mustard
2 spring onions, chopped
3 tbsp minced fresh dill
1 tsp olive oil
salt and pepper to taste

1 large chicken breast (skin removed), cooked and cubed
4 medium beetroot, cooked and diced (may use canned, drained beetroots)

Combine all the ingredients for the dressing – mustard, spring onions – dill, olive oil, salt and pepper – and whisk until well blended.

Mix the chicken cubes and the beetroot in a large bowl.

Pour the dressing over the chicken and beetroot, toss, and chill for several hours.

Serve.

GRILLED SEA BASS WITH DILL SAUCE

Serves 4

Sauce:
6oz/175g low-fat yogurt
2 tbsp chopped fresh dill
3–4 tbsp chopped gherkins
  (optional)
2 tbsp Dijon mustard
1 tsp fresh chopped tarragon

Fish:
4 x 8 oz fillets of sea bass
Fresh lemon juice
salt and pepper to taste

Sauce:
Combine all the ingredients in a small bowl. Whisk until thoroughly combined. Reserve.

Fish:
Preheat the broiler or grill. Sprinkle the fish with lemon juice and season with salt and pepper.

Grill until cooked through, about 3 minutes per side.

Serve with the sauce.

GRILLED HALIBUT WITH GREEN SAUCE

Serves 4

Green sauce:

1 bunch fresh parsley
1 bunch fresh coriander
4 garlic cloves, crushed
3 anchovy fillets

4 tbsp fresh lemon juice
3 tbsp olive oil
4 x 6-8 oz halibut fillets

Add all the ingredients for the sauce to a food processor and process until smooth. Reserve.

Cook on a barbecue or under a grill for about 4 minutes per side.

Serve with the green sauce.

NEW ORLEANS FETTUCCINE WITH MUSSELS

Serves 4

2 tbsp olive oil
1 medium onion, chopped
2 garlic cloves, crushed
1 tsp cayenne pepper
1 tsp paprika
1 tsp dried thyme
7oz/200g sliced fresh
   mushrooms

14oz/400g can of tomatoes
5oz/150g frozen peas
   (thawed)
24 fresh mussels, scrubbed
1lb/500g cooked Fettuccine
salt and pepper

Heat the olive oil in a saucepan. Add the onion, garlic and seasoning. Sauté for about 5 minutes. Add the mushrooms and cook for an additional 5 minutes. Add the tomatoes and simmer 10 minutes on a low heat, stirring constantly.

Stir in the peas and the mussels. Cover and cook, still on a low heat, until the mussels have opened. Season to taste.

In a large bowl, pour the sauce over the cooked pasta and serve immediately.

GOOD CALORIE CHICKEN SALAD

Serves 6

1lb/500g cooked skinless white-meat chicken, cubed
2 celery stalks, chopped
1 tbsp shallots, minced
3oz/75g grapes
2 tbsp chopped fresh dill
1 tbsp chopped fresh parsley
salt and pepper to taste
4oz/125g low-fat plain yogurt
salad leaves for garnish
sliced orange for garnish

Combine all the salad ingredients in a large bowl and chill. Serve on a bed of salad leaves with sliced orange.

MARINATED CHICKEN BREASTS

Serves 4

Marinade:

4 tbsp coarse-grain Dijon mustard

7 garlic cloves, crushed

4 tbsp fresh ginger, peeled and chopped

4fl oz/125ml soy sauce (wheat free)

4 tbsp sherry or cider vinegar

3 tbsp olive oil

2lb/1kg skinless chicken breasts

Whisk all the ingredients together in a small bowl.

Pour over the chicken breasts and marinate for at least 3 hours or overnight until chilled.

Discard the marinade and cook the chicken on a barbecue or under a grill until browned on both sides.

TURKEY CHILLI DIABLO

Serves 6–8

3 tbsp olive oil
1 large chopped onion
5 garlic cloves, chopped
2lb minced turkey
2 x 14 oz/400g cans of
  chickpeas or white beans
1 jalapeño chilli, seeded and
  chopped
2 pt/1.2L vegetable stock,
  or water

1 tbsp oregano
2 tbsp ground cumin
1 tsp basil
1 tsp marjoram
salt and pepper to taste
4fl oz/125ml water with
  1½ arrowroot,
  dissolved
chopped spring onions

In a large saucepan, heat the olive oil and sauté the onions and garlic until soft. Add the cumin and cook, stirring to release the spice's fragrance, for about 5 minutes.

Add the minced turkey, stirring to break it up, until the meat loses its pink colour. Add the chickpeas or beans, jalapeño chilli, vegetable stock or water, oregano, marjoram, and basil. Simmer, covered, for about 1 hour. Stir occasionally.

Add the arrowroot-water mixture and simmer for an additional 10 minutes.

Adjust the seasonings. Garnish with spring onions.

SPICY CHICKEN SALAD

Serves 4

Chicken Base:
2 whole chicken breasts,
   skinless and boneless
vegetable stock
1lb/500g good-quality
   spaghetti
salt and pepper to taste
chopped spring onions

Chilli Salsa:
4 large fresh tomatoes,
   chopped
1 tbsp jalapeño chilli,
   finely chopped
1 red onion, chopped
1 garlic clove, crushed
1 tsp lime juice
1 tsp salt

Salsa:
Combine all the ingredients in a bowl and mix well. Correct the seasonings. Cover and refrigerate.

Chicken Salad:
In a large saucepan, place the chicken and vegetable stock and bring to the boil. Add water, if necessary, to cover the chicken.

Simmer the chicken for about 10 minutes until tender. Cool the chicken, dice it, and reserve.

Cook the spaghetti in salted water, drain and set aside.

Combine the chicken, pasta and 2 cups of salsa in a large bowl.

Adjust the seasonings and add salt and pepper.

Serve at room temperature or chilled, with chopped spring onions for garnish.

PRAWNS WITH TOMATOES

Serves 4

2 garlic cloves, crushed
14 oz/400g can of Italian
   tomatoes
4 tbsp olive oil

12 jumbo prawns (about
   1lb/500g), peeled and
   deveined
4 tbsp dry white wine
   (optional)
salt and pepper to taste

In a nonstick saucepan, cook the garlic and tomatoes in 1 tablespoon of olive oil, stirring to prevent sticking, for about 15 minutes.

Heat the remaining oil in a large pan and sauté the prawns for 1–2 minutes until pink. Add the wine and heat. Deglaze the pan, scraping the browned bits.

Add the tomato mixture and heat until the prawns are cooked through. Season with salt and pepper to taste.

Serve with cooked rice or pasta.

MEXICAN CHICKEN FAJITAS
Serves 4

3 tbsp olive oil
1 green pepper, seeded and
    cut in narrow strips
1 red pepper, seeded and
    cut in narrow strips
1 large onion, thinly sliced
1lb/500g skinless, boneless
    chicken breasts, cut in strips
1 tsp ground cumin
salt and pepper to taste

Toppings:
chopped spring onions,
    cubed tomatoes, low-fat
    yogurt
soft cornflour tortillas

In a large, heavy pan, heat the olive oil, add the peppers and onion, and sauté until crisp-tender. Set aside. Add the chicken to the hot pan and sprinkle with cumin, salt and pepper. Sear the chicken, stirring until cooked through and sizzling. Return the vegetables to the pan just to heat. Serve the chicken and vegetables on tortillas topped with spring onions, tomatoes and yogurt.

ORANGE-GLAZED TURKEY BREAST

Serves 4

8fl oz/250ml orange juice   1 tsp sugar
2oz/50g fresh cranberries   1 tbsp olive oil
2 tbsp fresh rosemary,   4 turkey breast fillets
  chopped   salt and pepper to taste

Preheat the oven to 180°C/350°F. Heat the orange juice in a
saucepan and add the cranberries, rosemary and sugar.
Cook for about 15 minutes until the cranberries pop. Let
cool thoroughly. Purée the orange-berry mixture in a
blender or food processor. Season the turkey breasts with
salt and pepper. In a lightly oiled baking pan, roast the
turkey breasts until almost done, brushing with 1 teaspoon
olive oil to prevent drying. During the last 10 minutes of
cooking, brush the turkey breasts and the orange-berry
glaze, reserving some to serve as an accompaniment. The
breasts may also be cooked under the grill.

FLOUNDER WITH LEMON-MUSTARD SAUCE

Serves 4

4 tsp olive oil   pinch of cayenne pepper
2 shallots, finely chopped   1 tbsp coarse-ground
1 tbsp dried tarragon   mustard
4 tbsp cognac (optional, the   1 tbsp fresh lemon juice
  alcohol will cook away)   1lb flounder fillets
4fl oz/125ml tarragon vinegar

In a small nonstick saucepan, heat 2 teaspoons of the olive oil and add the shallots. Sauté the shallots until very soft for about 6–7 minutes. Add the tarragon, cognac, tarragon vinegar and cayenne pepper and cook until almost all the liquid has evaporated. Stir in the mustard and lemon juice and set aside.

Brush the fish fillets with the remaining oil and fry them quickly until they turn white and are cooked throughout. Serve the fish with a small portion of the lemon-mustard sauce.

PRAWNS WITH LEMON AND GINGER

Serves 4

2 tbsp olive oil   1lb/500g fresh prawns,
1 tbsp fresh ginger, chopped   peeled and de-veined
                                        (about 18 prawns)
                                     salt and pepper to taste
                                     juice of 1 large lemon

In a large pan, sauté the ginger in the olive oil until soft for about 6–7 minutes. Add the prawns and stir-fry until pink throughout. Season with salt and pepper. Transfer to a plate and drizzle lemon juice over the prawns.

SALMON AND BLACK BEAN SAUCE

Serves 4

3 tbsp canned black beans,
  drained
1 tbsp ginger, peeled and
  chopped
2 tbsp chopped onions
2 cloves of garlic, crushed

2 tbsp chives
1lb/500g salmon fillets
1 tsp sugar
2 tbsp cooking sherry
4 tsp sesame oil

Blend all the ingredients except the chives and salmon. Coat both sides of the salmon fillets with the mixture and refrigerate in a covered container until thoroughly cooled.

Cook under a preheated grill for 2 minutes. Turn and cook until the fish turns milky (2–3 minutes). Garnish with a light sprinkling of chives.

SIDE DISHES

BAKED TOMATOES

Serves 8

8 tomatoes
4fl oz/125ml tomato juice or
  vegetable juice
4oz/125g fresh 100 per cent
  rye-bread crumbs
4oz/125g low-fat yogurt
2 tbsp coarse-grained mustard

2 tbsp chopped fresh
  parsley
1 shallot, finely chopped
salt and pepper to taste
low-fat Parmesan cheese
  (optional)

Preheat the oven to 180°C/350°F/Gas Mark 4. Cut the tops off the tomatoes and remove the seeds.

In a mixing bowl, combine the tomato juice or vegetable juice, breadcrumbs, yogurt, mustard, parsley, shallot, salt and pepper. Stir to blend. Adjust the seasonings.

Spoon the mixture into the tomatoes and place in a lightly oiled baking dish.

Sprinkle with Parmesan cheese, if desired.

Bake for 25 minutes, or until hot and bubbly.

Serve.

BASMATI RICE AND SPLIT PEAS

Serves 6–8

3oz/75g yellow split peas
14oz/400g basmati rice
3 tbsp olive oil
½ tsp garam masala
1 tsp salt

4 tbsp chopped fresh dill
1¼ pt/750ml vegetable
   stock

Soak the split peas in hot water for 2 hours.

Soak the rice in water (2½ pt/1.5L) for 1 hour.

Drain the split peas and rice.

Heat the olive oil in a heavy saucepan and add the split peas
and rice. Stir-fry for a few minutes to coat with oil.

Add the garam masala, salt and dill.

Stir-fry for an additional 2 minutes.

Add the vegetable stock and bring to a boil. Reduce the heat
to low, cover, and cook gently for about 25 minutes.

Turn off the heat and allow to sit for 15 minutes, covered.

Serve.

WHITE BEAN AND GARLIC PURÉE

Serves 6–8

1lb/500g cooked or canned
   white or cannelloni beans
4 large garlic cloves, crushed

2 tbsp olive oil
salt and pepper to taste
1 tbsp fresh lemon juice

In a food processor combine the beans, 4fl oz/125ml bean liquid, garlic, olive oil, salt, pepper and lemon juice, and process until smooth.

Adjust the seasonings and add liquid, if necessary.

Heat over simmering water or in a double boiler.

Serve.

GOOD CALORIE VEGETABLE MEDLEY

Serves 6–8

7oz/200g yellow split peas
   (or lentils)
½ tsp turmeric
2½ pt/1.3L cold water
1 large tomato
1 tsp lemon juice
1½ tbsp olive oil
1 tsp black mustard seeds

¼ tsp fenugreek seeds
2 tsp garlic, chopped
1 tbsp garam masala
1lb/500g Brussels sprouts
8oz/250g green beans
2 tsp salt
2 tbsp chopped coriander
   leaves

Clean and wash the split peas. Combine the split peas, turmeric, and 1³/₄ pt/1L of the cold water in a large saucepan. Bring to the boil; reduce the heat to medium low; and cook for about 30 minutes until the split peas are tender. Add ¹/₄ pt/150ml water and continue cooking until the split peas are mushy. Remove from the heat.

Clean and wash the vegetables. Purée the tomato in a blender with the lemon juice and set aside.

In large saucepan heat the olive oil until very hot and add the mustard seeds. Add the fenugreek seeds and stir for approximately 1 minute until they start to darken. Add the garlic and garam masala. Add the vegetables and cook for 5 minutes. Add the reserved tomato purée, salt and an additional 4fl oz/125ml water. Cover the saucepan and cook over a low heat for 25 minutes. Add the split peas and stir. Continue cooking for 15 minutes until all the vegetables are tender. Stir in the coriander leaves. Correct the seasonings and serve.

FRESH BROCCOLI WITH LEMON VINAIGRETTE

Serves 4–6

1 large bunch fresh broccoli, trimmed
lemon slices (for garnish)

Dressing:
2 tbsp fresh lemon juice
1 tbsp white wine vinegar
1 tsp Dijon mustard
1 tbsp olive oil
1 tbsp fresh tarragon, chopped
salt and pepper to taste

Steam the broccoli until crisp-tender, and chill.

Whisk all the dressing ingredients in a small bowl.

At serving time, toss the broccoli with the vinaigrette and garnish with lemon, if desired.

COTTAGE CHEESE TOASTS

Serves 1

2 slices wholegrain or 100
   per cent rye bread
low-fat spread

2oz low-fat cottage cheese
cinnamon

Preheat the grill.

Spread the sliced bread with a thin coating of butter spread, top with cottage cheese, and sprinkle with cinnamon.

Grill about 10in/25cm from the heat, until warm and melted.

Serve immediately.

YELLOW PEPPER SAUCE

Serves 2

2 yellow peppers   4oz/125g low-fat yogurt
vegetable stock   salt and pepper to taste

Grill the peppers about 2in/5cm from the heat, turning frequently until the skins are blistered and charred. Transfer to a brown paper bag and leave until cool enough to handle. Peel off the skins and discard the ribs and seeds.

For the sauce combine the vegetable stock and peppers and simmer for 15 minutes. Stir in the yogurt. Cool.

Purée the mixture in a blender or food processor and process until smooth.

Season with salt and pepper.

Serve with grilled meats or fish.

CRANBERRY-GINGER-ORANGE RELISH

Makes 2 cups

2 tsp chopped fresh ginger   12oz/375g bag cranberries
1 large navel orange, peeled   1/4 tsp cinnamon
  and chopped

In a food processor, finely chop the ginger and orange. Add the cranberries and cinnamon and process until the berries are finely chopped. Chill and use as a condiment for meats and poultry.

DILL-YOGURT DIP

Makes 1 cup

8oz/250g plain low-fat   salt and pepper to taste
  yogurt
2 tbsp chopped fresh dill

Whisk the ingredients in a mixing bowl. Use as a dip for fresh vegetable crudités or as a garnish for Russian borscht.

TZATZIKI-GREEK CUCUMBER-YOGURT DIP

Makes 4 cups

1½lb/750g container
  low-fat plain yogurt
2 medium cucumbers
  coarsely grated
3 garlic cloves, chopped

2 tbsp olive oil
1 tbsp fresh dill
1 tbsp red wine vinegar
  or cider vinegar
pepper to taste

Place the yogurt in a very fine sieve over a bowl in the refrigerator overnight to drain the excess moisture.

Squeeze the cucumber to remove the excess liquid.

In a bowl, combine all the ingredients and add pepper to taste.

Serve with wholegrain bread or vegetable crudités.

STEWED TOMATOES AND OKRA

Serves 4–6

cooking spray
1 medium onion, chopped
4 tbsp green peppers, finely
  chopped
4 to 5 small okra, ¼ in/5mm
  slices
3 large tomatoes, coarsely
  chopped, seeds removed

¼ tsp hot pepper sauce
1 tsp dried ground oregano
1 tbsp lemon juice
salt to taste

Coat a frying pan with cooking spray and place over medium heat until hot. Add the onion and pepper and cook for 2 minutes, stirring constantly. Add the okra, tomatoes and remaining ingredients. Cover and cook over medium-low heat for 15 minutes or until the okra is tender. Stir occasionally.

PINTO BEAN DIP

Makes approximately 1¼ pt/750ml

14oz/400g can of white or plain pinto beans
1 green pepper, chopped
4 tbsp cider vinegar

1 jalapeño chilli, seeded and chopped
2 garlic cloves, crushed
½ tsp ground cumin
water, as needed

Place all the ingredients in a food processor bowl and process until smooth. Add water as needed. The mixture should be the consistency of a paste.

Use as a dip for vegetables, crackers or crisps.

SAVOURY BAKED YAMS

Serves 4–6

3 large yams, peeled and
  cubed
3 medium leeks (white and
  tender green parts only),
  thinly sliced

1 garlic clove, crushed
salt and pepper to taste
1 tbsp olive oil
¼ tsp ground sage

Coat a large piece of aluminium foil with olive oil to prevent sticking.

Place the vegetables and seasoning on the foil and wrap tightly.

Bake in a 200°C/400°F/Gas Mark 6 oven for 30 minutes or cook on a barbecue.

HORSERADISH DIP

Makes approximately 8fl oz/250ml

8oz/250g plain low-fat
  yogurt
2 tbsp horseradish (white)

2 tbsp ketchup
salt and pepper to taste
1 tbsp lemon juice

Mix all the ingredients well in a small bowl. Refrigerate. Serve with prawn cocktail or cold fish.

HORSERADISH AND BEETROOT PURÉE

Makes approximately 8 fl oz/250ml

8oz/250g beetroot,
  scrubbed and trimmed
2 tsp freshly grated
  horseradish, or strong white
  bottled horseradish

2 tsp red wine vinegar
salt and pepper to taste

In a large saucepan, cover the beetroot with water and bring to the boil. Simmer covered for 40 minutes, or until tender. Drain and skin the beetroot. In a food processor, purée the beetroot with the horseradish and vinegar. Add salt and pepper to taste.

Reheat in the saucepan over low heat before serving.

PURÉE OF BUTTERNUT SQUASH

Serves 6-8

1 large butternut squash
1 tbsp ground cinnamon
1/4 tsp nutmeg

4 tbsp cider
salt and pepper to taste

Preheat the oven to 180°C/350°F/Gas Mark 4.

Halve the squash lengthwise.

Peel and seed the squash and place the two halves, cut side down, in a large baking tin. Add about 1¹/² in of water.

Cover and bake for about 1 hour until the squash is very tender. Remove from the oven and cool slightly. Drain.

Purée the squash in a blender or food processor and then place the purée in a large bowl. Stir in the cinnamon, nutmeg, apple cider, salt and pepper.

Serve hot.

RICE PILAF

Serves 6–8

3 tbsp olive oil
1 tsp black mustard seeds
1 medium onion, chopped
1 tsp fresh ginger, finely
  chopped
4 garlic cloves, crushed
14oz/400g basmati rice
4oz/125g sliced mushrooms

2 tsp garam masala
1¹/² tsp ground coriander
salt and pepper to taste
1³/⁴ pt/1L boiling water
3 tbsp fresh parsley,
  chopped

Preheat the oven to 160°C/325°F/Gas Mark 3. Heat the olive oil in a large, heavy pan on high heat until hot. Add the mustard seeds and heat for a few seconds until they begin to pop. Add the onion and fry for about 5 minutes, or until lightly browned. Add the ginger and garlic and fry for about 1 minute.

Reduce the heat to medium low and add the rice,

mushrooms, garam masala, coriander, salt and pepper.
Sauté, stirring for about 10 minutes, until the rice turns
translucent and the vegetables are well coated with oil.

Add the boiling water and parsley. Turn the heat to high and
cook, stirring for about 5 minutes, or until most of the water
is absorbed. Cover tightly with aluminium foil, dull side
down, and then cover with the pot lid. Bake for 1 hour.
Serve hot.

SAFFRON RICE

Serves 4–6

3/4 pt/450ml vegetable stock
　or water
1/2 tsp salt
1 tbsp olive oil

1/4 tsp Spanish saffron
　threads
7oz/200g rice, washed

Bring the vegetable stock or water to a boil in a heavy
saucepan. Add the salt, olive oil and saffron. Reduce the
heat to low and add the rice, stirring with a fork. Cover
tightly and cook for about 15 minutes until the water is
absorbed.

SUGAR-FREE STRAWBERRY JAM

Makes approximately 1 pt/500ml

1lb/500ml fresh strawberries, sliced (or other fresh berries)
2 vanilla pods, split lengthwise
1 tbsp lemon zest

6fl oz/175ml frozen unsweetened white grape juice concentrate
4fl oz/125ml water

In a heavy saucepan, cook the strawberries, vanilla beans, lemon zest and grape juice concentrate until very thick. Stir frequently. Add water, if necessary, cooking for about 45 minutes. Remove the vanilla pods.

Remove from the heat, cool, and chill.

Store in the refrigerator for approximately 3 weeks.

Serve on cooked cereal, toast or yogurt.

FRUIT ICE OR 'GRANITA'

Serves 2

1¹/₄lb/625g unsweetened   4fl oz/125g water
   fresh fruit (berries,   1 tbsp fresh lemon juice
   pineapple, mango or   fresh mint leaves
   papaya)

Purée the fruit, water and lemon juice in a blender or food
processor. Freeze the mixture in an ice cream maker
according to the manufacturer's directions. Garnish with
fresh mint leaves before serving.

10

Eating in Restaurants

In this chapter, following a general discussion of each cuisine, you will find a list of menu items in which Good Calories and the least harmful Bad Calories are in bold face. Bad Calories are in regular type. Remember that these lists are based on approximations. Preparations and recipes vary, so you must use your judgement based on the guidelines in Chapters 3 and 4. Don't be afraid to ask your waiter for low-fat alternatives.

Some foods are followed by suggestions regarding alternative preparations that you can request. Avoid the foods described in the discussion as being Bad Calories. Remember to seek low-fat foods.

This list is *not* designed for people who eat every meal at a restaurant. Some of the choices are slightly too high in fat for continuous consumption. Millions of dieters know that it's not possible to eat out continually and lose weight. In other chapters the foods would be listed as Bad Calories. **You should use this list for the occasional treat.**

If you dine at a restaurant and innocently order a dish that is high in fat, do not panic. You can compensate by eating low-fat meals for the next day or two. Do not compensate by starving yourself.

If you are still treating the Starvation Response, you

should be extremely careful about what you eat. Do not use this list.

AMERICAN FOOD

This section does not include fast food. Instead, it refers to the typical food you will find at almost any restaurant that does not have an ethnic theme.

In many ways, it is easy to choose the proper foods in an American restaurant because the dishes do not generally contain unknown ingredients. If you follow the Golden Dozen rules, you cannot go wrong.

Remember, the biggest problems are combining starch and protein, eating bread before the meal, deep-fried foods, desserts, excessive protein, and high-fat foods.

STARTERS:

barbecued ribs
buffalo wings
calamari, deep fried
cheese, deep fried
chicken nuggets
clams, fried

deep-fried vegetables
escargots
mussels, steamed
oysters on the half shell
potato skins

SALADS:

avocado salad
avocado, stuffed
Caesar salad
chicken tostada salad
fruit salad
green salad with low-fat dressing

spinach salad with low-fat dressing
tomato and onion
tortilla salad
turkey salad with low-fat dressing

SOUPS:

borscht (no sour cream)
chicken noodle
chicken rice
corn chowder
cream of asparagus
cream of chicken
cream of mushroom
lentil

lobster bisque
clam chowder
onion soup with cheese
onion soup without cheese
split pea
vegetable

MAIN DISHES:

barbecued chicken, the sauce on the skin, which should be avoided
barbecued ribs
beef stew
blackened fish
blackened steak

Chicken à la king
chicken fried steak
chicken, no skin
chicken, Southern fried
chilli, beef
chilli, chicken or bean
corned beef hash

crab cakes

crabs, soft shelled

filet mignon

fish and chips

fish, broiled, from an acceptable fish listed in the seafood section

fish, deep fried

fish, grilled, from an acceptable fish listed in the seafood section

flank steak, not marinated

ham

hot dogs

jambalaya

lamb

lasagne

liver

lobster

pasta, no cream sauce

prime rib

quail

rib roast

spaghetti

spareribs

steaks, beef, except those listed

veal chop

CHINESE FOOD

Chinese food is really a variety of cuisines: Cantonese, Szechuan, Beijing, Hunan, Shantung, Honan, Shanghai and others. There are three major styles of preparation: deep frying, stir-frying, and steaming. Deep-fried foods are Bad Calories because of the fat. Steamed foods are almost always Good Calories. Stir-fried foods, which predominate, can be either Good Calories or Bad Calories, depending on their fat content.

Although Chinese fast food is almost universally high in fat and salt, you can still get a great healthy meal at a Chinese restaurant. I live outside San Francisco, and one of my favourite evenings out is to eat in Chinatown. I concentrate on steamed foods and eat smaller portions, along with lots of steamed rice.

Styles of rice preparation also vary. Watch out for the glutenous rice that is featured in some restaurants and has a high glycaemic index. You should also avoid rice that is cooked so that the kernels stick together, making it easy to eat with chopsticks. Since this kind of rice is prevalent in Chinese restaurants, you should be very careful about eating rice.

Egg rolls, fried shrimp, fried wontons, fried dim sum, pork strips, tofu (bean curd), sweet fried foods and sour sauces, sweet sauces, bird's nest, plum sauce, cashews, peanuts, duck and beef should all be avoided. This means that almost all the appetizers are off-limits. You might make sure that vegetable oils are used for cooking. Fortunately, peanut and sesame oils are prevalent.

On the positive side, Chinese cuisine features rice, vegetable dishes and Chinese noodles (not fried noodles), all of which are Good Calories.

STARTERS:

chicken wings	prawn balls
dim sum, fried	sesame prawns on toast
dim sum, steamed, no tofu	spareribs
egg rolls	spring rolls
fried prawns	**steamed vegetarian and**
fried wontons	**seafood dim sum**
pork strips	

SOUPS:

chicken and asparagus,
    combination (pork, chicken
    and beef)
crab meat and asparagus
hot and sour soup

**sam shin (noodles, chicken,
    seafood and vegetables)**
shark fin
shredded pork
sizzling rice
watercress
wonton soup

MAIN DISHES:

barbecued spareribs
bean curd
beef and broccoli
braised pork
cashew shrimp
chicken and cashews
chicken with bamboo shoots
chicken with broccoli
chicken with chestnuts
chop suey
chow mein
crab meat and eggs
crispy beef or pork
crispy whole fish
deep-fried chicken, seafood
    or beef
**drunken chicken, marinated
    in wine**
duck

egg dishes
**eggplant (without meat
    sauce)**
fried food
fried rice with chicken,
    seafood, pork or beef
goose
hot and sour shrimp
Hunan chicken
lamb
**lo mien (noodles), chicken,
    vegetable or seafood**
lobster
lychee chicken
**Moo Goo Gai Pan (sautéed
    chicken)**
mushrooms and broccoli
panfried noodles
poached fish

pork

pork sausage

pork, barbecued

pork, roast

prawns, sautéed

prawn with broccoli

prawn with tomato sauce

sizzling beef

spareribs

spicy green beans

steamed chicken

sweet and sour chicken,

   pork and shrimp

Szechuan beef

Szechuan fish

tofu (bean curd)

twice-cooked pork

vegetarian stir-fry

FAST FOOD

The greatest problem in compiling a list of fast-food Good Calories is that restaurants are constantly adding new low-fat menu items. It is simply impossible to keep up with the tens of thousands of possible items, most of which are Bad Calories. In any case, you should be careful, since not all low-fat items are Good Calories. Many are high in blood sugar-inducing carbohydrates and should be rejected.

This section lists only generic fast-food items. Foods with a fat content of less than 31 per cent are in bold face; foods with a fat content of 31 per cent to 40 per cent are also in bold face, but they are followed by an asterix. Pizza is perhaps the best fast food when it is low in fat.

Fast-food items, such as sandwiches and pizza, combine protein and starches. This combination raises their fat-forming capacity. There are two ways to combat this problem. First, make sure that you do not eat other carbohydrates, such as chips or milk-shakes, with sandwiches or pizza. Second, you should realize that sandwiches tend to be Bad Calories because they combine starches and protein; therefore, you should eat them only as part of a controlled programme. These meals should be followed and preceded by several days of Good Calorie meals.

GENERIC FAST-FOOD ITEMS:

cheeseburger
chicken fillet, fried
chicken, grilled*
chicken, breaded
chicken nuggets
chilli
chips
clams, fried
coleslaw
cookies
crab, baked*
crisps
croissant
egg and cheese
fish fillet
fizzy drinks
**fizzy drinks artificial
   sweetener**
French toast
ham and cheese
ham, egg and cheese
hamburger, large
hamburger, small*
   (moderate fat, but

**combines protein and
   starch)**
hot chocolate, milk based
**hot chocolate, water based
   and sugar free**
hot dog
hush puppies
ice cream
juice, grapefruit
juice, orange, no sweetener
juice, orange, sweetener
juice, tomato
lemonade
milk
milk shakes
onion rings
oysters, fried
pancakes
pie, fruit
pizza, cheese*
pizza, meat
potato salad
potato, baked
roast beef* **(moderate fat,**

and starch)
roast beef and cheese
salad, cheese and egg, no
    dressing
salad, chef, no dressing
**salad, green, with low-fat
    dressing**
salad, seafood pasta, no
    dressing
**salad, vegetable, with
    low-fat dressing**

**but combines protein
salad, with prawn and
    low-fat dressing**
sausage
scallops, fried
prawn, fried
prawn, grilled
**steak sandwich• (moderate
    fat, but combines protein
    and starch)**
turkey, club sandwich

FRENCH AND
CONTINENTAL-STYLE FOOD

Classic French food is high in saturated fats, primarily because butter is used so liberally. However, the 'nouvelle' French cuisine, which originated in health spas, has steered away from the excessive use of fat. Almost all French restaurants now feature elements of the nouvelle cuisine. Therefore, choosing the proper foods is as simple as discarding much of the classic cuisine and determining what foods are nouveau and therefore probably low in fat. Any good waiter will be glad to help you make this decision.

Remember that certain classes of French food are high in fat. Avoid heavy sauces (béchamel, bearnaise, cheese, cream, hollandaise and Mornay), cheeses, goose, duck, sausage, lamb and beef.

STARTERS:

artichoke with butter or
vinaigrette sauce
caviar
cheese
confit of duck
escargots

fondue
grilled asparagus
grilled shrimp
mussels au gratin
pâté
terrine

SOUP:

bisques
bouillabaisse
broth (bouillon)

consommé
cream soups
onion soup without cheese

SALAD:

**fresh seafood salad (not in a
mayonnaise dressing)**
**green salad (generally
acceptable if without
cheese and in a light
dressing)**
**house salad (generally
acceptable if without
cheese and in a light
dressing)**

marinated tomatoes
**niçoise (do not eat the egg
yolk)**
seafood salad with
mayonnaise
**spinach salad (generally
acceptable if without
cheese or bacon and in
a light dressing)**

MAIN DISHES:

beef wellington

blackened fish

bouillabaisse

braised fish (with no or low-fat topping)

brochette of chicken

chicken Kiev

coq au vin

Dover sole

duck

filet mignon aus jus (with no or low-fat topping)

grilled chicken (with no or low-fat topping)

grilled fish

poached fish

rabbit (lapin) (with no or low-fat topping)

rack of lamb

sautéed chicken (with no or low-fat topping)

steaks, rib eye, and sirloin

sweetbreads

ITALIAN FOOD

Italian cuisine is really two different styles. The southern style is heavy on pasta and tomato sauces. The northern style resembles a lighter version of French cooking and is considered to be one of the world's great cuisines. This discussion focuses on the southern style simply because it is more common.

An increasing number of Italian restaurants serve olive oil with bread. This combination lowers the glycaemic index of the bread. However, you should avoid eating too much or you will consume too much fat.

Remember, pizza can be a Good Calorie food. Avoid deep-dish pizzas, which tend to be higher in fat. You should also avoid an excess of cheese; double cheese is forbidden. Play it safe and request lighter-than-normal cheese. You should also avoid fatty toppings, such as sausage and pepperoni. Vegetable toppings, except olives, are a good bet. If the pizza is made with unsaturated oils, then it can be a great choice.

Pasta is an excellent choice, but avoid eating too much protein with it. Stuffed pasta is frequently filled with high-fat ingredients or cheese; avoid it. I don't recommend pesto either. Order a light sauce, in a minimal quantity.

Avoid all breaded and deep-fried foods. Also avoid foods with cheese toppings, such as veal and eggplant parmigiana. Most risotto dishes are high in fat and cheese; substitute a rice-vegetable combination.

STARTERS:

antipasti di molluschi (assorted shellfish)

antipasto

bruschetta (grilled bread)

calamari, deep fried

calamari, in tomato sauce

calamari, marinated

carciofi al forno (artichokes baked with oil)

capriccio (paper-thin sliced beef)

clams, steamed

cozze della riviera (mussels in red sauce)

eggplant, baked with cheese

funghi marinati (marinated mushrooms)

garlic bread

peperonata (pimentos, onions, and tomato sautéed in oil)

peperoncini arrostiti (roasted peppers)

pizza, no excess of cheese or meat

pompelmo (grapefruit)

prosciutto

sarde all'olio (sardines in oil)

SOUPS:

brodetto pasquale (meat vegetables, and egg yolks)

brodo (broth)

busecchinia (chestnuts and milk)

cassola (fish stew)

crema (cream soup)

lentil

lentil and sausage

minestrone

panata (bread with cheese)

pasta e fagioli (bean and pasta)

ribbollita (vegetables with bread)

stracciatella fiorentina (Italian chicken soup with dumplings)

wedding soup

zuppa alla marinara (fish stew)

zuppa di cozze (mussel soup)

zuppa di fagioli ed orzo (bean and barley)

zuppa di pesce (fish)

zuppa di spinaci (spinach)

zuppa di vongole (clams steamed in wine)

zuppa pavese (topped with cheese and egg)

SALADS:

arugula and Belgian endive

Caesar salad

insalata composta (mixed salad)

insalata cotta (cooked vegetable salad)

insalata di casa (house salad)

insalata di fagiolini (green bean salad)

insalata di gamberi (prawn)

insalata di limone, cetriolo, e peperone (lemon, cucumber and pepper)

insalata di patate con la pancetta affumicata (potato salad with bacon)

seafood, marinated on greens

seafood, on greens

tortellini salad with pesto

MAIN DISHES:

agnolotti

aragosta fra'diavolo (lobster braised in wine)

arrosto alla bolognese (roast chicken with ham)

bigne di peci misti (deep fried seafood)

bistecca (beef steak)

brazino alla griglia (grilled snapper)

brodetto (fish stew)

calamari barcaiola (squid in wine sauce)

calzone (folded pizza, limit cheese and meat fillings)

cannelloni (stuffed pasta)

capelli'angeli (angel-hair pasta)

cappe saltare (sautéed scallops)

cassola (fish stew)

chicken cacciatori (chicken in mushrooms, tomatoes, and herbs; be careful because the sauce can be full of fat)

chicken in wine sauce (with no pasta accompaniment)

chicken parmigiana

costoletta di pollo (chicken breast, ask about preparation)

cozze a vapore (steamed mussels)

egg dishes

eggplant parmigiana

fagioli (white beans)

fettuccine alle vongole (clam pasta, limit the fat content, no cream sauce)

filetti di tacchino (turkey-breast slices)

gamberetti (small prawns)

gnocchi (pasta filled with starches)

lasagne

manicotti (pasta stuffed with cheese)

medaglioni di bue (filet mignon)

molecche (soft-shell crabs)

pasta ai quattro formaggi (pasta with four cheeses)

pasta al marscarpone (creamy pasta)

pasta all'uovo (egg pasta)

pasta e ceci (pasta and chickpeas)

pasta e fagioli (pasta and white beans)

pasta primavera (if not heavy with cream or cheese; ask)

pasta with Bolognese sauce

pasta with cheese or cream
sauces
pasta with tomato sauce and/
or minimal cheese
pece passera (flounder)
pece spada alla griglia
(grilled swordfish)
pizza al pomodoro (pizza
with tomato sauce and
no cheese)
pizza al rosmario (pizza with
rosemary)
pizza vegetale (pizza with
vegetables)
pizza, with meat or excess
cheese
pizza, with vegetables and
limited cheese
polenta
pollo al vino bianco
(chicken in white wine;
ask if it is low fat and
make sure olive oil is
substituted for butter)
pollo alla cacciatori (chicken
in mushrooms, tomatoes
and herbs; be careful
because the sauce can be
full of fat)
pollo alla griglia (grilled
chicken)
pollo alla zingara (chicken
baked in a clay pot)

pollo arrostio (roasted
chicken)
pollo di forno (baked
chicken; avoid the
skin)
pollo in picatta (chicken
sautéed in olive oil)
ravioli (stuffed pasta)
risotto (rice with butter
and cheese)
riso (rice, with low-fat
toppings)
sarde (sardines)
scallops Marsala
scampi
scampi al vino bianco
(prawns sautéed in wine;
request that the dish is
cooked in olive oil, not
butter)
scampi fra'diavolo (prawns
in tomato sauce)
seafood, grilled, poached or
baked
shrimp marinara
shrimp primavera (if not
heavy with cream or
cheese)
shrimp scampi
spaghetti (with low-fat
sauce)
spaghetti alla carbonara
(pasta with bacon, butter
and egg)

tacchino arrosto (roast
   turkey, white meat only)

tetrazzini (chicken or turkey
   casserole)

veal

JAPANESE FOOD

The Japanese have a longer life expectancy than do people in other industrialized countries – perhaps the longest in the world. Japanese women live to be 81 years old, on average. One reason for this longevity may be that the Japanese diet is one of the best low-fat Good Calorie diets.

Almost all Japanese dishes are Good Calories. There are only a few significant problems. Avoid eating too much rice with animal protein. Sushi (cold rice wrapped around fish or vegetables) should not be mixed with sashimi, in which fish is the main ingredient. Avoid tempura and agemano dishes because they are deep fried and generally high in fat.

Some sushi and sashimi dishes feature fish that are excessively high in fat. Therefore, I will comment on a list of the Japanese names for the various fish ingredients.

Although salt is not directly linked to weight loss unless you suffer from water retention, you should be aware that soy sauce, shoga (the pickled ginger that is served with every meal) and teriyaki are high in salt.

Tofu is high in fat and should be avoided. Miso soup is tofu based and should also be avoided.

Finally, the February 1987 bulletin of the Food and Drug Administration in the United States

recommended against eating raw fish, such as that
found in sushi and sashimi because a disease called
anisakiasis can result from parasites that are
sometimes found in raw fish.

STARTERS:

agedashi tofu
ebi-su (prawn)
gyoza (fried dumplings)
kani-agemano (fried crab)
kushiyaki (chicken on a
  stick)
ohitashi (spinach with
  soy sauce)

oshinko (pickled
  vegetables)
shumai (steamed prawn
  dumplings)
tempura
yakitori (teriyaki chicken
  skewers)

SOUPS:

miso
susmashijiru (clear broth)
susmono (clear broth)

tempura-udon (tempura
  with noodles)
yaki udon (noodles with
  vegetables)

SALADS:

cucumber and seafood with
  vinegar dressing
seafood sunomono (seafood
  with vegetables in
  vinegar dressing)

tofu salad with miso
  dressing
tossed salad with miso
  dressing
wakame-su (seaweed and
  cucumber)

MAKI, SUSHI AND SASHIMI:

aji (mackerel)
amaebi (sweet prawn)
anago (eel)
awabi (abalone)
California maki (crab and
    avocado)
ebi (prawn)
hirame (halibut)
ika (squid)
ikura (salmon egg)
kainahira (scallop)
kaki (oyster)
kani (crab)
kappamaki (cucumber)

magura (dark tuna)
masago (smelt egg)
saba (mackerel)
sake (salmon)
**shinkomaki (pickled
    radish)**
tako (octopus)
tamago (poultry egg)
tobiko (flying-fish egg)
toro (fatty tuna meat)
**umekyumaki (plum and
    cucumber)**
unagi (freshwater eel)

MAIN DISHES:

agemano (breaded and deep-
    fried crab)
**donburi (low-fat course
    over rice; avoid tempura
    and teriyaki)**
**shabu-shabu (sliced beef
    cooked at the table)**
**soba (buckwheat noodles
    with anything that is low
    in fat; no tempura)**
sukiyaki (ask for no tofu)

tempura
teriyaki
tofu dishes (dengaku,
    hiyayakko, iridofu,
    mabodofu, yudofu)
**udon (noodles with
    anything that is low in
    fat; no tempura)**
udon sauté
**yosenabe (noodles,
    vegetables and seafood)**

MEXICAN FOOD

Mexicans are genetically susceptible to the Starvation Response, so it makes sense that they would develop a Good Calorie cuisine. Beans appear in most dishes and will lower the glycaemic index of the entire meal. Mexican food is also good in that it does not stress high-protein dishes.

Unfortunately, the restaurant version of Mexican food is frequently high in fat. Animal lard is dripped onto beans and meat, making it hard to eat healthily in some restaurants. Many foods are deep fried. Avoid foods such as taco shells, and substitute tortillas that are not fried, such as soft tacos and enchiladas. Ask your waiters about the preparation.

The use of saturated animal fats is particularly troubling. Some Mexican restaurants may offer special low-cholesterol meals. These dishes will probably be lower in fat and feature unsaturated vegetable oils. Ask your waiter to go easy on the sour cream, guacamole, deep-fried chips, fried tortilla shells, hard taco shells, cheese, bacon, chorizo (Spanish sausage), and refried beans, since these foods are high in fat.

STARTERS:

almejas al vapor (steamed clams)
melted cheese
baked chips with salsa
ceviche (marinated fish)
chips with guacamole or
deep-fried chips with salsa
pescado espada y melon en brocheta (kebab of fish and melon)
nachos
tostada chips, deep fried
tostada chips, oven baked

SOUP:

black bean (without sour
cream)

gazpacho (without sour
cream)

SALADS:

dinner salad (without
cheese; use salsa for

Mexican salad (without
cheese and do not eat the
tortilla shell, or ask for a
soft corn tortilla for the
shell and salsa for the
dressing)
taco salad

MAIN DISHES:

arroz con pollo (boneless
chicken on rice; excessive
starch with protein)
burritos, meat
burritos (without high-fat
refried beans or cheese)
camerones de hacha
(prawn in tomato sauce)
carne asada
chicken chimichangas
(without high-fat refried
beans or cheese)

chicken enchiladas
(without high-fat refried
beans or cheese)
chicken fajitas (avoid
guacamole, cheese, and
sour cream)
flautas con crema
mole pollo
tacos
tortillas (corn)
tostadas

SIDE DISHES:
_____

black beans	rice (if not in a protein-rich meal)
guacamole	
refried beans	salsa
	tortilla chips (baked only)

SEAFOOD

Seafood is the fastest-growing segment of the restaurant market. It is usually a low-fat alternative to red meat. Charcoaled, grilled, raw broiled, sautéed in wine sauce, steamed and kebabed seafoods are generally good choices.

However, you should be careful, since many of the most popular seafood dishes are as high in fat as red meat. Butterfish, catfish, caviar, mussel and salmon are all Bad Calories, even when grilled.

Many methods of seafood preparation create Bad Calories. Many seafoods, such as shrimp, lobster and tuna salads are full of fatty mayonnaise. Deep-fried fish, clams, prawns and crabs are Bad Calories. Creamy sauces, stuffed fish and casseroles are generally high in fat. Remember to avoid combining seafood with starches, such as rice or potatoes.

Fast-food seafood shops are full of the worst Bad Calories. All their breaded and deep-fried foods should be avoided. If they have a grilled or baked alternative, take it.

Salmon is increasingly available as farm-bred salmon flood restaurants and stores. Many of these salmon have a high fat content. It is generally better to eat wild salmon, which get more exercise.

STARTERS:

calamari, fried
calamari, marinated
calamari, steamed
clam fritters
raw clams

raw oysters
**raw sashimi (if the fish is a
    Good Calorie)**
shrimp cocktail
steamed clams
tempura

SOUPS:

bisque, shrimp or lobster
bouillabaisse

gumbo

MAIN DISHES:

abalone
alewife (herring)
anchovy
anchovies (canned)
barbecued prawn
bass, black
bass, freshwater
bass, striped
bluefish
butterfish
clams, steamed

carp
carp, fried
carp, roe
carp, smoked
casserole
catfish
caviar
chub
clams, breaded and fried
clams, canned
lobster, Newburg

cod
cod, frozen, raw
crab salad
crab, devilled
crab, imitation
crab, king
crab, soft shell, fried
crayfish
cuttlefish
dogfish
eel
fish and chips
flounder
flounder, baked with butter
flounder, baked, no butter
flounder, raw, frozen
gefilte fish
grouper
haddock
haddock, breaded and fried
halibut, batter fried
halibut, broiled with butter
halibut, grilled, no butter
halibut, raw
halibut, smoked
herring
herring, kippered
jambalaya (avoid the
    sausage)
kebabs (see listings for
    individual seafood)
king crab
lobster, grilled or
    broiled

mackerel
mackerel, canned
monkfish
mussel
octopus
oyster stew
oysters, breaded and fried
oyster, canned
oyster, fresh
paella (avoid the sausage)
perch, breaded and fried
perch, freshwater
perch, ocean
pies, lobster or other
    seafood
pike
rockfish
salmon cake
salmon, Atlantic
salmon, pink, canned
salmon, smoked
sardines
scallops
scallops, breaded and fried
scrod
sea bass
sea trout
seafood creole
shad
shark
prawns
prawns, canned
smelts
snapper

sole   tuna, canned in oil
stuffed fish   **tuna, canned in water**
swordfish (trimmed of fat)

THAI FOOD

Thai cuisine, when properly prepared, is low in fat and meat and features vegetables, seafood, rice and rice pasta that are Good Calories. It is easy to maintain the Good Calorie Diet while enjoying frequent Thai meals.

Coconut milk is the most fattening ingredient of Thai cooking. It is not the clear juice found in coconuts, but white pulp mashed into a paste. Not only is it extremely high in fat (97 per cent), but it is composed of saturated fats that resemble animal fats. Thus, it easily induces the Starvation Response. Coconut milk is found in many soups, such as Tom Ka Gai and curries. Avoid dishes that contain coconut milk. Don't eat these dishes even during a Bad Calorie splurge.

Animal lard and coconut oil are used for stir-frying in the rural areas of Thailand. Although most Thai restaurants use vegetable oils, I have found a few that cling to traditional ways. Ask your waiter.

The other major problems are with deep-fried items and nuts. Consult the discussion of Chinese food and apply those principles to Thai cuisine.

STARTERS:

satay (meat or chicken marinated in coconut milk)

seafood kebab (if you are not having a rice-laden entrée)

steamed mussels

Tao Hoo Tod (fried tofu)

Thai rolls

Tod mon (fish cake)

Tod mun (deep-fried seafood)

SOUPS:

Poh Taag (hot-and-sour seafood)

Tom Ka Gai (chicken with coconut)

Tom Ka Pak (vegetable with coconut)

Tom Yum Gai (hot-and-sour chicken)

Tom Yum Koong (lemon grass and shrimp)

SALADS:

Laab (meat salad)

Pla Goong (charbroiled prawn salad)

Pla Koong (prawn salad)

spiced beef salad

Talay Thong (chilli seafood)

Thai salad

yam yai (combination salad)

Yum Pla Muk (calamari salad with lemon juice)

Yum Saw Menu (eggplant salad)

Yum Yai (Thai green salad without the egg)

MAIN DISHES:

beef, basil
chicken, basil
chicken, tomato sauce
chilli beef
curry, green, red, yellow, or
   Mussaman (curry sauce
   is in many dishes; ask)
deep-fried fish
duck dishes
Gai Him Ma Pan (cashew
   chicken)
Gai Pad Khing (ginger
   chicken)
Gai Pad Praw (basil
   chicken)
Gai Yang (barbecued
   chicken, discard the skin
   and eat only the white
   meat)
Gang Pug (vegetable curry)
Goong Choop Pang (fried
   prawns)
Goong Gra Tiem (garlic
   prawns)
Goong Ob Maw Din (clay-
   pot prawns)
Goong Pea Seau (fried
   prawns with crab stuffing)
Gra Praw Neau (basil beef)
Moo Pad Ma Keau (eggplant
   pork)

Moo Yang (barbecued pork)
Nea Yang (barbecued beef)
Neau Pad Nam Mon Hoy
   (oyster beef)
Pad Jay (rice noodles and
   vegetables)
Pad Kao Pod (corn beef)
Pad Kao Pod (corn chicken)
Pad Kao Pod (corn pork)
Pad Ma Keau (sautéed
   eggplant)
Pad Thai Jai (noodles with
   prawn, tofu and egg)
Pad Thai Jai (noodles with
   tofu and egg)
Pad Sai Roong (rice
   noodles with tofu)
Pad Thai (rice noodles and
   shrimp; without the
   peanuts)
peanut sauces
Pla Laad Prik (fried whole
   spicy fish)
Pla Muk Choop Pang (fried
   calamari)
Pla Muk Gra Praw (basil
   sautéed calamari)
Pla Song Kreug (deep-fried
   whole fish)
Praram long song (beef with
   curry)

Pug Raum Mit (sautéed
   mixed vegetables)
scallops
seafood platter (without
   curry sauce)

spinach with peanut sauce
Thai chicken
tofu

11

Glycaemic Indexes of Common Foods

This chapter lists the glycaemic indexes of foods that are known to have been measured. Most of you will never use these figures, but will rely on chapter 12 to tell you what foods are Good or Bad Calories, which is generally all you need to know.

However, there are two situations, both of which involve a variation of the basic simple programme in which these figures may be of use to you. If you are cheating on your diet and want to counter Bad Calories with the best possible Good Calories, then you may wish to consult this list to find the foods with the lowest glycaemic indexes. If you are combining caloric restriction with Good Calories, then you will also want to know which are the best possible Good Calories.

One note of caution in interpreting these numbers: just because a food has lower glycaemic index than sugar (78) does not necessarily mean that it is a Good Calorie. Foods with unacceptably high fat contents can also have low glycaemic indexes. Clearly, they are not Good Calories. Use your judgment.

Remember that glycaemic indexes do not measure the total blood sugar that will be produced by a given food but rather how efficient one calorie is in producing an increase in blood sugar. Thus it is not necessary to specify the quantity of food to use these numbers.

MEASURED INDEXES OF FOODS

Food	Glycaemic Index
Breads	
Barley, coarse	57
Barley, coarse, scalded kernels	48
Barley, whole meal	93
crackers, plain	100
oat, coarse	93
rye, crisp bread	95
rye, pumpernickel	68
rye, whole grain	42
rye, whole meal	89
wheat, whole meal	100
wheat, coarse	73
wheat, French baguette	131
wheat, puffed crisp bread	112
wheat, white bread	100
Pasta	
macaroni, white, boiled 5 minutes	64
spaghetti, white, boiled 15 minutes	67
spaghetti, brown, boiled 15 minutes	61
spaghetti, white, boiled 5 minutes	45
spaghetti, protein enriched	38
star pasta, white, boiled 5 minutes	54
Cereal Grains	
barley, pearled	36

Food	Glycaemic Index
buckwheat	76
bulgur	65
couscous	66
millet	103
rye kernels	47
sweet corn	80
wheat kernels	63
wheat kernels, quick cooking	75
wheat kernels, steamed	41

Rice and Rice Products
bran	31
brown	81
Chinese glutenous rice	98
waxy rice, boiled 14 minutes	120
white, instant, boiled 1 minute	65
white, instant, boiled 6 minutes	121
white, parboiled, boiled 15 minutes	68
white, parboiled, boiled 5 minutes	54
white, polished, boiled 5 minutes	58
white, polished, boiled 10–25 minutes	81

Breakfast Cereals
40% bran flakes	104
All Bran	74
Cornflakes	121
muesli	96
oat bran	85
oats, rolled	85
oatmeal, long cooking	49
porridge oats	89
puffed rice	132
puffed wheat	122

Food	Glycaemic Index
Rice Krispies	112
Shredded Wheat	97
Weetabix	109

Desserts

custard	55
digestive biscuits	82
oatmeal	78
rich tea biscuits	80
shortbread	88
sponge cake	46
ice cream	80
tofu ice cream substitute	155
ice cream, high fat	36

Root Vegetables

beetroot	64
carrot	92
parsnip	97
potato, instant	120
potato peeled, sliced, and microwaved	117
potato, mashed	98
potato, white (new), boiled	80
potato, russet, baked	116
sweet potato	59
yam	62

Legumes

baked beans, canned	70
black-eyed beans	33
butter beans	46
chickpeas, dried	47
chickpeas, canned	60
dhal, Bengal gram lentils	12

Food	Glycaemic Index
haricot beans	40
green peas, dried	50
green peas, frozen	65
kidney beans, dried	43
kidney beans, canned	74
lentils, green, dried	33
lentils, green, canned	74
lima beans	36
pinto beans, dried	60
pinto beans, canned	64
peas, dried	49
peas, frozen	51
peanuts	15
soya beans, dried	20
soya beans, canned	22
white beans, Haricot, dried	54

Ethnic Foods and Meals

Greek: lentils and bread	54
Italian: spaghetti Bolognese	70
East Indian: lentils and rice	81
Chinese: glutenous rice	98
Lebanese: bread and chickpeas	116

Fruit

apple	46
apple juice	45
apple sauce	41
apricots	94
banana, green	56
banana, ripe	90
cherries	23
grapes	45

Food	Glycaemic Index
grapefruit	26
mango, ripe	81
orange	54
orange juice	65
papaya, ripe	81
peaches	29
pears	34
plums	25
raisins	93

Sugars	
fructose	25
glucose	138
honey	106
lactose	57
maltose	152
sucrose	78

Dairy Products	
custard	59
skimmed milk	39
whole milk	41
yogurt	44

Snack Foods	
corn chips	99
crisps	68
tomato soup	38

12

Good and Bad Calories, by Category

Good Calories are in bold face. Bad Calories are in regular type. Bad Calories followed by an asterisk (*) have 31 per cent to 40 per cent fat and are suitable for occasional use, as the best Bad Calories to use after you have overcome the Starvation Response.

Bakery items	Legumes
Beverages	Meat
Breakfast cereals	Nuts
Condiments	Pasta
Dairy products	Poultry
Fish	Rice dishes
Fruit, fresh	Sugars
Fruit, canned	**Vegetables, fresh**
Fruit, frozen	Vegetables, canned

BAKERY ITEMS

Wheat flour is one of the greatest sources of Bad Calories, since it causes up to twice as much blood sugar as sugar does. There are almost no bakery products that are acceptable in the Good Calorie Diet.

Rye flour has a lower blood sugar-producing potential. Rye breads, such as pumpernickel, are generally acceptable. However, you must make sure that rye flour is the dominant ingredient.

bagels	**cake, sponge**
biscuits	crackers, plain
BREAD	crisp bread rye
corn	crisp breads
rye, crisp bread	croissant
rye, pumpernickel	croutons
rye, whole grain	croutons, cheese
rye, whole meal	Danish pastry
wheat, diet	doughnut
wheat, French	matzo
baguette	matzo meal
wheat, puffed crisp	muffins
bread	pies, fruit and nut
wheat, whole meal	rolls
wheat, white bread	**rye kernels**
	rye, whole grain

BEVERAGES

As a general rule, juicing fruits or vegetables will only increase the blood sugar-producing potential of the ingredient. The physical forces involved in juicing destroy the fibres that are essential for lowering the amount of blood sugar it produces. Therefore, if the fruit or vegetable is a Bad Calorie, it will be an even worse juice.

Many beverages have added sugar, and such drinks usually have too high a blood sugar-producing potential.

During the Good Calorie Diet, you should

minimize your intake of caffeine. When possible, drink caffeine-free beverages.

If you are going to drink beer, drink low-calorie beers that have a high chromium content (see Chapter 5).

apple cranberry drink
apple drink
apple juice, unsweetened
apple cranberry juice
apricot nectar
beer, lite
beer, normal
berry drinks
carrot juice
cherry drink
**cherry juice,
   unsweetened**
cider
cocoa
fruit drinks
fruit punch
grape juice, red
**grape juice,
   unsweetened**
grapefruit juice,

unsweetened
grapefruit juice,
   sweetened
lemonade
orange drink
orange juice, sweetened
**orange juice,
   unsweetened**
papaya nectar
passion fruit juice
peach nectar
pineapple juice,
   sweetened
**pineapple juice,
   unsweetened**
raspberry-cranberry
   drink
soft drinks
soft drinks, diet
tomato juice

BREAKFAST CEREALS

Most breakfast cereals are Bad Calories. There are three reasons for their high fat-forming potential. First, many cereals are made with wheat flour, a Bad Calorie. Second, many cereals have a high sugar content. Finally, many cereals have been processed so much (into flakes or puff balls) that their fibre content is destroyed.

Oat cereals are one of the few types of Good Calorie cereals. However, it is important that they not be overly processed. For example, instant oatmeal is unacceptable whereas regular oatmeal is a Good Calorie.

All Bran	oat bran, flaked
Cornflakes	**oatmeal, long cooking**
granola	oatmeal, instant
hominy	oats, rolled
muesli	porridge oats
oat bran cereal	puffed rice
oat bran flakes	puffed wheat
oat bran, dry, 100 per cent	Rice Krispies
	Shredded Wheat

CONDIMENTS

The only key to these products is their fat content. Very few have high blood sugar-producing potential.

Mayonnaise should be avoided since diet mayonnaise is still too high in fat content, and the non-dairy mayonnaises made with tofu or soybean oils are Bad Calories.

barbecue sauce	mayonnaise
béarnaise sauce	mayonnaise, light
carob chips	**mustard**
carob powder	**salsa**

DAIRY PRODUCTS

In this category, fat content is the problem. If you look carefully, you will see that most of the acceptable choices are followed by an asterisk, indicating that they have a fat content of 31 per cent to 39 per cent. These products should be avoided until you cure the Starvation Response and used sparingly thereafter.

On the other hand, just because a dairy product may have a high fat content does not mean that you cannot use it for cooking. As an ingredient, it forms such a small part that the resulting dish is low fat.

butter
butterfat
cheese, all, except those
   that are low in fat
cottage cheese, all, except
   those that are low in fat
cream cheese, all
cream, all
eggs, chicken

eggs, duck
eggs, quail
ice cream, all, except
   low-fat varieties
margarine
sherbet
sorbet

FISH

Many of the most popular fish are high in fat, including crab, mussels, pompano, roughy, and some salmons.

abalone*
alewife (herring)*
anchovy
anchovy, canned

bass, black
bass, freshwater
bass, striped
bluefish*

butterfish
carp
carp, fried
carp, roe
carp, smoked*
catfish
caviar
chub
clams, breaded and fried
clams, canned
clams, steamed
cod
cod, frozen, raw
crab, deviled
crab, king
crab, soft shell, fried
crayfish
cuttlefish
dock
dogfish
eel
flounder
gefilte fish, in broth
grouper
haddock
haddock, breaded and
  fried
halibut, raw
halibut, smoked
herring
herring, kippered
lobster*
mackerel

monkfish
mussel
octopus
oyster, breaded and fried
oyster*
perch, breaded and fried
perch, fresh water
perch, ocean
pike
pompano
rockfish
roughy
sable fish
salmon, **Atlantic**
salmon, fish farm
salmon, pink, canned*
sardines
scallops
scallops, breaded and fried
scrod
sea bass
sea trout*
shad
shark*
sheepshead
shrimp
shrimp, canned
smelt
snapper
sole
tuna, canned in oil
tuna, canned in water

FRUIT

Avoid dried fruits because the process of drying concentrates the sugar. Soaking does not help.

Bananas induce one-third more blood sugar than sugar. However, if you eat bananas that are not totally ripe, there is some suggestion that the induced blood sugar will be much lower.

apple	**kiwifruit**
apricot, dried	**lemon**
apricot, fresh	**lime**
banana	**mandarin orange**
blackberry	**mango**
blueberry	**nectarine**
boysenberry	**orange**
cantaloupe	**papaya**
casaba melon	**peaches**
cherries	**pears**
dates	pineapple
figs, dried	**plums**
figs, fresh	prunes
grape	raisins
grapefruit	watermelon
honeydew melon	

FRUIT, CANNED

Canned fruits are Good Calories as long as they are not overcooked or packaged in syrup. Many baby foods are processed into a paste that may be acceptable for babies but are Bad Calories for adults.

**applesauce, natural
   (unsweetened)**
applesauce, sweetened
**apricot, natural
   (unsweetened)**
apricot, sweetened
blackberry, in syrup
blackberry, in water
blueberry, in water
blueberry, sweetened
cherries, in water
**cherries, maraschino,
   unsweetened**
cherries, in syrup
figs, in syrup
figs, in water
fruit cocktail, in syrup
fruit cocktail, in water
fruit salad, in syrup
fruit salad, in water
jam and jelly, sweetened
**jam and jelly,
   unsweetened**
mandarin orange, in
   syrup
**mandarin orange, in
   water**
peaches, sweetened
peaches, unsweetened
pears, sweetened
pears, unsweetened
plums, sweetened
plums, unsweetened
prunes

FRUIT, FROZEN

Avoid any frozen fruit packaged in syrup.

blackberry, in syrup
blackberry, in water
blueberry, in water
blueberry, sweetened
cherries, in water
cherries, in syrup
raspberry, in syrup
raspberry, in water
rhubarb
rhubarb, sweetened

LEGUMES

Legumes are probably the best food for people on the Good Calorie Diet. They often have less than half the blood sugar-producing potential of sugar. By adding them to a meal, you can drastically reduce that meal's fat-forming potential.

Combining 1 unit of legumes to $2^1/2$ units of grain (rice or corn) produces a perfect protein that supplies all the body's needs. If you are trying to maximize your weight loss by avoiding meat products, this combination is a great substitute.

aduki beans, boiled	kidney beans, dried
aduki beans, canned	lentils, green canned
aduki beans	lentils, green dried
beans, baked, canned	lima beans
black bean soup	moth beans
black-eyed beans	mung bean sprouts
butter beans	peanuts
chickpeas, canned	peanut butter
chickpeas, dried	pinto beans, canned
chilli beans	pinto beans, dried
dhal lentils	soya beans, canned
green peas, dried	soya beans, dried
green peas, frozen	white beans, Haricot,
haricot beans	dried
kidney beans, canned	

MEAT

These listings are based on the most commonly sold grades of meat. The higher grades of meat are also the highest in fat, which enhances their taste. However, it is possible to raise animals so they produce less fat. You may be able to find more kinds of cuts of beef and other meats at speciality stores.

Do not confuse 'health food' meats with low-fat products. Health food stores often feature meats that may not contain as many chemicals as regular products, but contain just as much fat.

BEEF
  blade
  brisket, lean
  chuck, no fat
  club steak, lean*
  corned beef
  flank, lean
  ground, lean
  kidneys
  liver*
  porterhouse, no fat
  rib eye
  rib roast
  ribs
  round, bottom, no fat*
  round, eye, no fat*
  round, full cut, no fat*
  round, tip, no fat*
  round, top, no fat
  rump roast, no fat*
  sirloin, lean*
  T-bone
  tenderloin
  tongue
  top loin

hot dogs
KIDNEYS
  beef
  lamb
  pork
  veal
LAMB
  chops
  foreshank
  ground
  kidneys
  leg, roast
  liver
  loin
  ribs
  shank
  shoulder
  sirloin
LIVER
  beef
  lamb
  pork
  veal
PORK
  all except those listed

arm, lean roasted
ham, extra lean
heart
kidney
lean tenderloin
liver
loin
ribs
tenderloin, roasted,
   lean
rabbit, wild
rabbit, domestic
VEAL
   breast

chop
chop, lean only*
chuck
cutlet
cutlet, lean only
heart*
kidneys
liver
loin
ribs
round
rump
sweetbreads
tongue*

NUTS

Nuts are popular with health food advocates, but are very high in fat. Soaking does not help.

acorn
acorn flour
almond butter
almond powder,
   defatted*
almond powder, normal
almond
Brazil nut
butternut
cashew
cashew butter
chestnut
coconut milk

coconut water
coconut, sweetened
coconut, unsweetened
coconut, whole
filbert
macadamia
peanut
peanut, dry roasted
pecans
pine nuts
pistachio
walnut

PASTA AND PASTA SAUCES

Do not overcook.

clam sauce, red
clam sauce, white
**macaroni, white, boiled
5 minutes**
noodle dishes
noodles, egg
**spaghetti, brown, boiled
15 minutes**

**spaghetti, protein
enriched**
spaghetti, white, boiled
15 minutes
**spaghetti, white, boiled
5 minutes**
**star pasta, white, boiled
5 minutes**

POULTRY

The Good Calorie Diet is like any other diet when it comes to poultry. Choose low-fat portions. Skin-free breasts, white meat, and skin-free drumsticks are the best choices.

Always separate protein-rich foods from starchy carbohydrates. When possible, eat protein at lunch and eat other foods two hours before or after it.

CAPON
  skinned, dark meat
  skinned, white meat
  whole
CHICKEN
  back, no skin
  breast with skin*
  breast, no skin
  breast, smoked*
  chicken roll, light

luncheon meat
chicken salad
dark meat, no skin
drumstick with skin
drumstick, no skin*
fried
leg, no skin
roasting, whole
  roasted*
stewing, whole

thigh, no skin
thigh, with skin
white luncheon meat*
white meat, no skin
wing, no skin*
wing, with skin
DUCK
  domesticated
  liver*
  wild, meat only*
GOOSE
**guinea hen, meat only
  (no skin)**
guinea hen, whole*
pheasant
quail, breast
quail, whole
TURKEY
  breast roast*
  breast slices
  breast tenderloins
  back meat only*
  **breast, fillet, without
    skin**
  breast, half, without
    skin
  **breast, slices, without
    skin**
  breast, cooked*

dark meat without
  skin*
dark meat with skin
**dark meat without
  skin**
drumsticks
drumsticks without
  skin*
giblets, simmered
gizzard, simmered
heart, simmered
**light meal without
  skin**
light meal with skin*
liver, simmered
meat and skin, dark
  and light, no giblets
  or neck
**meat only, light and
  dark**
thighs without skin
thighs with skin
whole turkey
wing drumettes
wing drumettes
  without skin*
wings
wings without skin

SUGARS

fructose

glucose

honey

lactose

maltose

molasses

sucrose (table sugar)

VEGETABLES, FRESH

acorn squash

alfalfa sprouts

aloe vera juice

artichoke

asparagus

aubergine

avocado

avocado dip

bamboo shoots

bean sprouts

beet greens

beetroot

broccoli

brussel sprouts

butternut squash

cabbage

carrot

cauliflower

celery

coleslaw

corn, sweet

cranberry

cucumber

endive

green beans

Jerusalem artichoke

kale

leek

lettuce

mushroom

mustard greens

okra

olives

onions

parsnip

peas

**peppers, sweet, green
    and red**

POTATO

  peeled, sliced and
        microwaved

  instant

  mashed

  russet, baked

  white, boiled, new

radish   squash
rhubarb   sweet potato
rocket   tomato
spinach   yam
spring greens

VEGETABLES, CANNED

Canned vegetables are Good Calories as long as they
are not overcooked. Many baby foods are processed
into a paste that may be acceptable for babies but are
Bad Calories for adults.

artichoke hearts,   cucumber, pickled
  marinated   green beans
asparagus   kale
baby food   kidney beans
bamboo shoots   mushroom
bean dip   mustard green
bean salad   okra
bean sprouts   olives
beans   onions
beetroot   peas
black-eyed peas   pickles
butter beans   pinto beans, canned
butter beans, with pork*   potato
Chinese vegetables   refried beans
collards   refried beans, low fat
corn   sauerkraut
cranberry   tomato paste
cranberry sauce

Appendix 1

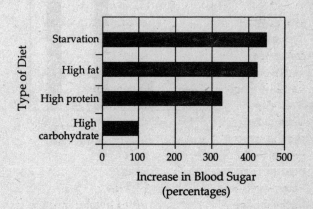

FIGURE 2-1

Blood Sugar After Different Diets
(Smaller Responses Are Better)

FIGURE 2-2

*Increase in Triglyceride Levels as the
Starvation Response Develops
(Smaller is Better)*

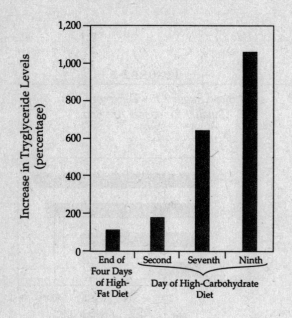

FIGURE 2-3

*Lipoprotein Lipase Activity in the
Presence of Excess Fat
(Smaller is Better)*

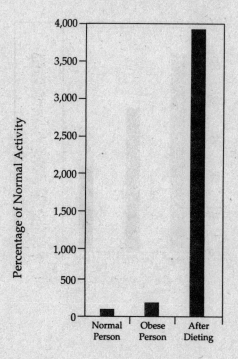

FIGURE 3-1

*Decreasing Amount of Calories from Good Calorie
Carbohydrates in our Diet*

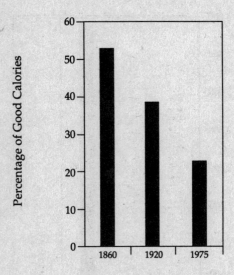

FIGURE 3-2

*Glycaemic Index After Equal Amounts of Saturated
and Unsaturated Fats Are Added to Bread
(Smaller is Better)*

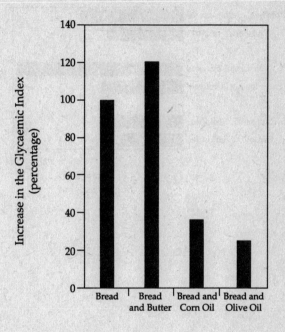

FIGURE 3-3

*Blood Sugar Created by Equal Portions of Rice
by Type of Rice and Different Cooking Times
(Smaller Responses Are Better)*

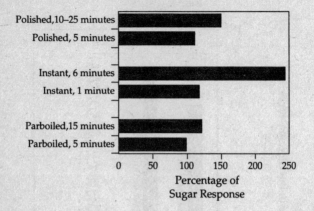

Percentage of
Sugar Response

FIGURE 3-4

Insulin Levels After Five Weeks of Consuming
Different Amounts of Fructose Sweetener
(tested one-half hour after Test Carbohydrates
were ingested)
(Smaller is Better)

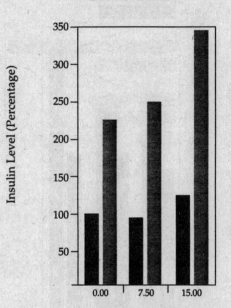

Amount of Fructose Sweetener
(percentage)

■ Normal
▨ Starvation Response

FIGURE 3-5

Triglyceride Levels in Men After Five Weeks of
Consuming Different Amounts of
Fructose Sweetener
(Smaller is Better)

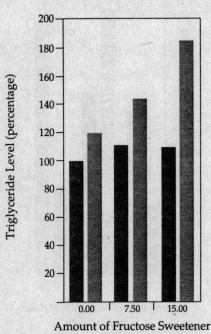

FIGURE 7-1

*Concentrations of HDL (Fat-Forming) Triglycerides
with Good and Bad Calories in People Suffering from
the Starvation Response (Smaller is Better)*

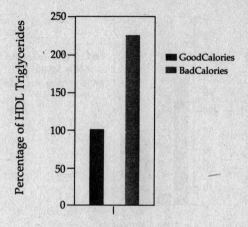

FIGURE 7-2

*Increase in Blood Sugar after Eating
Good and Bad Calorie Potatoes
(Smaller is Better)*

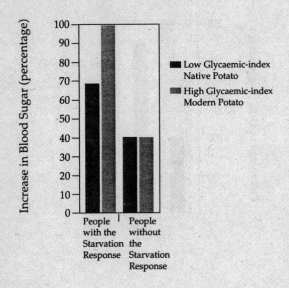

FIGURE 7-3

*Increase in Insulin after Eating
Good and Bad Calorie Potatoes
(Smaller is Better)*

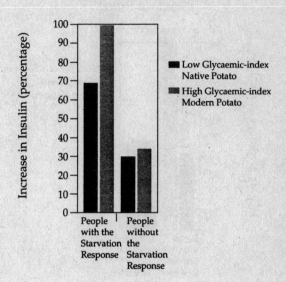

FIGURE 7-4

HDL Triglycerides
(The Most Fat-Forming Triglycerides)
After Eating Good and Bad Calorie Potatoes
(Smaller is Better)

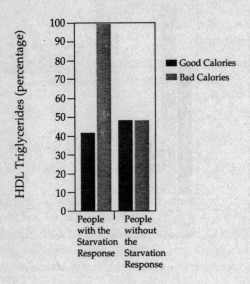

Appendix 2

Historical Perspective

They are as sick that surfeit with too much as they that starve with nothing.

WILLIAM SHAKESPEARE (1564-1616)
The Merchant of Venice, 1, ii

This is how *The Surgeon General's Report on Nutrition and Health* (1988) opens its discussion of obesity:

Historians of obesity, finding new scientific records, have searched for clues in linguistics, history and art and have concluded that obesity as it is now known did not occur in England, except in a few isolated instances, until it began to appear in the English upper classes in the 18th and 19th centuries.

One hypothesis suggests the ability to store excess calories as fat in adipose tissue was useful during prehistoric times as a protection against food shortages. However, the ability later became a handicap in industrialized societies.[1]

The report makes quite clear what many people have always known in their hearts – that modern eating habits are the source of excess fat. The problem has been that, until now, no one knew exactly what were the dangerous elements of the modern diet. Without this information, it is nearly impossible to correct the problem. Clearly, you can not abandon everything just to eliminate a few harmful elements.

It is my hope that the Good Calorie Diet has given you the freedom to enjoy modern food, without the anxiety that you are eating the wrong foods. In this respect, it has been my intention to create a diet of freedom. If you enjoy yourself as you return to health, then you will have fulfilled my fondest wish.

Thank you for taking this journey with me.

Write to me about your experiences:

Box 322

20 Sunnyside

Mill Valley, CA 94965

U.S.A.

I cannot promise to acknowledge all correspondence, but I will read as many letters as possible. I may use your story or suggestion in a future book. I am also interested in the experiences of alcoholics, drug users, and people with either mental or eating disorders.

Source Notes

1.

1. F. X. Pi-Sunyer, *Nutrition* 7: 292-94 (1991).

2.

1. J. S. Sweeney, *Arch. Internal Med.* 40: 818-30 (1927).
2. H. P. Himsworth, *Clin. Sci.* 67-94 (1935).
3. *Nutrition Reviews* 49: 364-66 (1991).
4. K. J. Acheson et al., *Am J. Clin. Nutr.* 48: 240-47 (1988).
5. D. M. Mott et al., *Metab. Clin. Exp.* 35: 160-65 (1986); L. Tappy et al., *Diabetes Care* 14: 1180-88 (1991); J. F. Caro et al., *Diabetes Metab. Rev.* 5: 665 (1989); and J. P. Felber et al., *Diabetes* 36: 1341-1350 (1987).
6. R. Schmid et al., *J. Clin. Endocrinol. Metab.* 68: 1106-1110 (1989); and P. Damsbo et al., *Diabetologia* 34: 239-45 (1991).
7. F. X. Pi-Sunyer, *Nutrition* 7: 292-94 (1991).
8. P. Martin et al., *Metabolism* 36: 1154-64 (1988); J. P. Flatt, *Ann. NY Acad. Sci.* 499: 104-23 (1987); K. J. Acheson et al., *Am. J. Clin.* 48: 240-47 (1988); and S. J. Bhathena et al., *European J. Clin. Nutr.* 42: 465-72 (1988).
9. K. J. Acheson et al., *Am. J. Clin. Nutr.* 48: 240-47 (1988).

10. T. J. Yost and R. E. Eckel, *J. Clin. Endocrinol. Metab.* 67: 259-64 (1988).

11. Ibid.

12. R. S. Schwartz and J. D. Brunzell, 'Recent Advances in Obesity Research: III' (1981).

13. N. B. Ruderman, *Am. J. Clin. Nutr.* 34: 1617-21 (1988); S. Lillioja et al., *J. Clin. Endocrinol. Metab.* 73: 866-76 (1991); J. V. Neel, *Am. J. Hum. Genet.* 14: 353-62 (1962); G. Reaven, *Diabetes* 37: 1595-1607 (1988); and J. F. Caro, *J. Clin. Endocrinol. Metab.* 73: 691-9 (1991).

14. J. S. Romijn et al., *Metabolism* 39: 525-30 (1990); R. Schmid et al., *J. Clin. Endocrinol. Metab.* 68: 1106 (1989); A. Franssila-Kallunki et al., *Metabolism* 40: 689-94 (1991); G. C. Cook, *Metabolism* 17: 1073-83 (1968); G. C. Cook, *Nature* 215: 1295-96 (1976); W. P. T. James and H. G. Coore, *Am. J. Clin. Nutr.* 23: 386-89 (1970); and J.-P. Felber, *Int. J. Obesity* 16: 937-52 (1992).

15. D. Porte and S. C. Woods, *Diabetologia* 20: 274-80 (1981).

16. I. J. Stein et al., *Endocrinology* 113: 299-301 (1983); and J. Rodin et al., *Metabolism* 34: 826-31 (1985).

17. S. J. Bhathena et al., *Proc. Soc. Exp. Biol. Med.* 181: 71-77 (1986); R. Schmid et al., *J. Clin. Endocrinol. Metabol.* 68: 1106 (1989); Y. B. Lombardo et al., *Horm. Metab. Res.* 25: 69-76 (9183); and N. Geary, *Neuroscience Behav. Rev.* 14: 323-38 (1990).

18. R. P. S. Kwok and A. V. Juorio, *Neuroendocrinol.* 45: 267-73 (1987); R. J. Wurtman and J. J. Wurtman, *Appetite* 7 (Suppl.): 88-103 (1986); D. V. M. Ahsley et al., *Am. J. Clin. Nutr.* 42: 1240-45 (1985); S. Paykfl et al., *Br. J. Psychiat.* 123: 501-07 (1973); and I. Blum et al., *Am. J. Clin. Nutr.* 57: 486-89 (1993).

19. F. K. Hamalainen et al., *J. Steroid Biochem.* 20: 459-64 (1984); and B. R. Goldin and S. L. Gorbach, *Am. J. Clin. Nutr.* 48: 787-90 (1988).
20. G. M. Reaven, *Diabetes* 37: 1595-1607 (1988).

3.

1. H. C. Burkett and H. C. Trowell, *Western Diseases: Their Emergence and Prevention* (1981).
2. L. H. Storlin et al., *Am. J. Physiol.* 251:E583 (1986).
3. B. A. Swinburn et al., *J. Clin. Endocrinol. Metabol.* 73: 156-65 (1991); and J. A. Marshall et al., Am. J. Epidemiol. 134: 590-603 (1991).
4. A. Astrup and A. Raben, *Eur. J. Clin. Nutr.* 46: 611-20 (1992); and D. H. Ekwyn et al., *Am. J. Clin. Nutr.* 32: 1597-1611 (1979).
5. J. E. Blundell and V. I. Bruley in *Progress in Obesity Research*, eds. Oomura, Y et al. London: John Libbey, 453-57 (1990).
6. M. C. Gulliford et al., *Am. J. Clin. Nutr.* 50: 773-77 (1989); E. Gatti et al., *Eur. J. Clin. Nutr.* 46: 161-66 (1991); and G. Collier et al., *Diabetologia* 26: 50-54 (1984).
7. C. R. Sitori et al., *Am. J. Clin. Nutr.* 44: 635-42 (1986).
8. E. Gatti et al., *Eur. J. Clin. Nutr.* 46: 161-66 (1991).
9. P. J. H. Jones et al., *Metabolism* 37: 145-51 (1988).
10. P. J. H. Jones et al., *Metabolism* 41: 396-401 (1992); L. Forsgren, *Arch. Kemi* 30: 355-60 (1968); and J. B. Watkins et al., *Gastroenterol.* 82: 911-2717 (1982); and P. J. H. Jones et al., *Am. J. Clin. Nutr.* 42: 769-77 (1985).
11. S. W. Mercer and P. Trayhurn, *J. Nutr.* 117:2147-53 (1987); and P. J. H. Jones et al., *Metabolism* 41: 396-401 (1992).
12. P. J. H. Jones et al., *Metabolism* 41: 396-401 (1992).

13. K. Hermansen et al., *Diabetic Medicine* 9: 739-43 (1992); and T. M. S. Wolever et al., *J. Clin. Nutr. Gastroenterol.* 3: 85-88 (1988).

14. J. D. Brand et al., *Am. J. Clin. Nutr.* 42: 1192-96 (1985).

15. J. Holm et al., *Eur. J. Clin. Nutr.* 46: 629-40 (1992).

16. G. R. Herxberg and M. Rogerson, *J. Nutr.* 118:1061-67 (1988).

17. H. L. Higgins, *Am. J. Physiol.* 41: 258-65 (1916).

18. G. R. Herxberg and M. Rogerson, *J. Nutr.* 118: 1061-67 (1988).

19. J. Hallfrisch et al., *J. Nutr.* 113: 1819-26 (1983); S. Resier et al., *Am. J. Clin. Nutr.* 45: 580-87 (1987); and A. W. Thorburn et al., *Am. J. Clin. Nutr.* 49: 1155-63 (1989).

20. J. Hallfrisch et al., *Am. J. Clin. Nutr.* 37: 740-48 (1983); and J. Hallfrisch et al., *J. Nutr.* 113: 1819-26 (1983).

21. Ibid.

22. Ibid.

23. J. V. Selby et al., *Am. J. Epidemiol.* 125: 979-88 (1987); D. T. Fowman, *Ann. Clin. Lab. Sci.* 18: 181-89 (1988); and M. J. Gerald et al., *Diabetes* 26: 780-85 (1977).

24. Lancet (October 30, 1965).

25. P. Felig, et al., *JAMA* 242: 1591 (1979); O. Pederson, *New England J. Med.* 302: 886-92 (1980); and D. M. Klatchko et al., *Diabetes* 21: 89-100 (1972).

26. D. L. Costill et al., *J. Appl. Physiol: Respirat. Environ. Exercise Physiol.* 43: 695-99 (1977); G. K. Grimditch et al., *Am. J. Clin. Nutr.* 48: 38-43 (1988); J. E. Donnelly et al., *Am. J. Clinc. Nutr.* 54: 56-61 (1991); R. J. Harvel et al., *J. Appl. Physiol.* 23: 90-99 (1967); and C. Oster et al., *Med. Sci. Sports* 11: 1-5 (1979).

27. C. Connell, *Associated Press* (July 30, 1993).

28. J. C. Cohen and R. Hickman, *J. Clin. Endocrinol. Metab.* 64: 960-63 (1987).

4.

1. D. J. A. Jenkins et al., *Diabetes Care* 11: 149-59 (1988).
2. D. J. A . Jenkins et al., *BMJ* 297: 958-60 (1988).
3. R. N. Podel and W. Proctor, *The G-Index Diet.* New York: Warner Books (1993).
4. L. J. D. O'Donell et al., *BMJ* 298: 1616-17 (1989).
5. P. R. Ellis et al., *Br. J. Nutr.* 46: 267-76 (1981).
6. D. J. Scholfield et al., *Am. J. Clin. Nutr.* 46: 955-61 (1987).
7. Quoted in B. Lehamn, *Marin Independent Journal* D1 (September 13, 1993).
8. H. Liljeberg et al., *Eur. J. Clin. Nutr.* 46: 561-75 (1992).
9. T. M. S. Wolever et al., *Diabetes Care* 9: 401-04 (1986).

5.

1. J. E. Nester et al., *Diabetes Care* 11: 755-60 (1988).
2. D. J. A. Jenkins et al., *Am. J. Clin. Nutr.* 35: 1339-46 (1982).
3. A. S. Levine et al., *Am. J. Clin. Nutr.* 50: 1303-7 (1989); and J. E. Blundell et al., *Int. J. Obesity* 11 (Suppl. 1): 9-25 (1987).
4. T. M. S. Wolever et al., *Am. J. Clin. Nutr.* 48: 1041-47 (1988).
5. J. Bertelsen et al., *Diabetes Care* 16: 4-7 (1993).
6. R. Schmid et al., *J. Clin. Endocrinol. Metab.* 68: 1106 (1989); G. B. Forbes, *Am. J. Clin. Nutr.* 52: 224-27 (1990); J. C. Floyd et al., *J. Clin. Invest.* 45: 1476-86 (1966); D. Estrich et al., *Diabetes,* 16: 232-37 (1967);

D. Rabinowitz et al., *Lancet* 2: 454-57 (1967); Spiller et al., *Am. J. Clin. Nutr.* 46: 474-80 (1987); R. Schmid et al., *J. Clin. Endocrinol. Metab.* 68: 1106-10 (1989); and P. J. Crowe and G. T. Royle, *J. Nutr.* 118: 1240-44 (1988).

7. M. C. Gullford et al., *Am. J. Clin. Nutr.* 50: 773-77 (1989).
8. O. Rasmussen et al., *Metabolism* 42: 214-17 (1993).
9. W. C. Rose, *J. Biol. Chem.* 217: 997-1004 (1955).
10. J. M. Whitaker, *Reversing Diabetes.* New York: Warner Books (1987).
11. A. De Burgos et al., *Eur. J. Clin. Nutr.* 46: 803-08 (1992); R. A. DeFronzo, *Metabolism* 37: 105-08 (1988); and J. Kersteer et al., *Metabolism* 40: 707-13 (1991).
12. C. J. Schorah et al., *Internat. J. Vit. Res.* 58: 312-18 (1988).
13. E. Altenburger, *Klinishe Wochenschrift* 15: 1129-31 (1936).
14. C. G. King, *J. Biol. Chem.* 116: 489-92 (1936); S. Banerjee, *J. Biol. Chem.* 168: 207-11 (1947); and S. Banners, *Nature* 152: 152 (1943).
15. J. Kersteer et al., *Metabolism* 40: 707-13 (1991).
16. O. Geddik and S. Akalin, *Diabetolgica* 29: 142-45 (1986).
17. G. Paolisso et al., *Am. J. Clin. Nutr.* 57: 650-56 (1993).
18. J. Durlach et al., *Magnesium* 2: 192-224 (1983); and G. Paolisso et al., *Diabetes Care* 12: 265-69 (1989).
19. R. Baltzan et al., *J. Clin. Invest.* 41:108-14 (1962); P. J. Kesterns et al., *Metabolism* 12: 941-50 (1963); and R. A. DeFronzo et al., *Am. J. Physiol.* 238: E421-E427 (1980).
20. D. Rabinowitz and K. L. Zierler, *J. Clin. Invest.* 41: 2173-81 (1962); and R. A. DeFronzo, *Metabolism* 37: 105-8 (1988).

21. National Academy of Sciences, National Research Council, *Recommended Dietary Allowances* (9th ed.). Washington, DC: National Academy Press (1980); L. M. Klevay et al., *JAMA* 241: 1916-18 (1979); and J. M. Holden et al., *J. Am. Dietetic Assoc.* 79: 23-28 (1979).

22. S. J. Bhathena et al., *Eur. J. Clin. Nutr.* 42: 465-72 (1988).

23. P. J. Charley et al., *Biochem. Biophysc. Acta* 69: 313-21 (1963); M. Fields, et al., *Am. J. Clin. Nutr.* 39: 289-95 (1984); M. Fields et al., *J. Nutr.* 113: 1335-45 (1983); S. Reiser et al., *Am. J. Clin. Nutr.* 38: 214-22 (1983); and S. Reiser et al., *Am. J. Clin. Nutr.* 42: 242-51 (1985).

24. R. A. Anderson and A. S. Kozlovsky, *Am. J. Clin. Nutr.* 41: 1177-83 (1985).

25. R. A. Anderson et al., *Am. J. Clin. Nutr.* 51: 864-68 (1990); W. Mertz, *Physiol. Rev.* 49: 163-239 (1969); and R. A. Anderson, *Clin. Physiol. Biochem.* 4: 31-41 (1986).

26. L. L. Hopkins et al., *Am. J. Clin. Nutr.* 21: 203-11 (1968); R. A. Levine et al., *Metabolism* 17: 114-25 (1968); W. H. Glinsmann and W. Mertz, *Metabolism* 15: 510-15 (1966); E. Glaser and G. Halpern, *Biochem Z.* 207: 377-83 (1929); W. Mertz, in *Present Knowledge in Nutrition* 365-72 (1976); R. A. Anderson, *Metabolism* 36: 351-55 (1987); R. A. Anderson et al., *Am. J. Clin. Nutr.* 54: 909-16 (1991); R. W. Truman and R. J. Doisy, in *Trace Elements Metabol. in Animals* – 2. Hoekstra, JW 678 (1974); and A. S. Abraham et al., *Metabolism* 41: 768-71 (1992).

27. R. G. Lefavi et al., *Inter J. Sports Nutr.* 2: 111-22 (1992); R. J. Moore and K. E. Friedl, *Nat. Strength Cond. Assoc. J.* 14: 47-51 (1992); P. M. Clarkson, *Inter*

J. Sports Nutr. 1: 289-93 (1991); R. G. Lefavi, Inter J. Sports Nutr. 3: 120-21 (1993); M. A. Hallmark et al., Med. Sci. in Sports & Exercise 25: S101 (1993); S. Clancey et al., Med. Sci. in Sports & Exercise 25: S194 (1993); C. J. Seal, Ann. Nutr. Methol. 32: 186-91 (1988); D. L. Hasten et al. (conference abstract) S. E. Regional Chapter, Am. College of Sports Med. (1991); J. A. Fernandez-Pol and G. S. Johnson, Cancer Res. 37: 4276-79 (1977); and K. R. Etzel et al., Nutr. Res. 8: 1391-1401 (1988).

28. M. Urberg and M. B. Zemel, Metabolism 36: 896-99 (1987); R. W. Squires et al., Mayo Clin. Proc. 67: 855-60 (1992); R. Lefavi et al., FASEB J. 5: A1645 (1991); and M. Urberg et al., J. Family Practice 27: 603-06 (1988).

29. J. E. Nester et al., Diabetes Care 11: 755-60 (1988).

6.

1. B. Linde et al., Am. J. Physiol. 256: E12-E18 (1989).

2. E. Hagstrom-Toft et al., J. Clin. Endocrinol. Metabol. 76: 392-98 (1993).

3. C. R. Kahn et al., Endocrinol. 10: 1054, 1066 (1978); and R. H. Rao et al., Metabolism 40: 1292-97 (1991).

4. R. H. Rao et al., Metabolism 40: 1292-97 (1991); W. P. T. James and H. G. Coore, Am. J. Clin. Nutr. 23: 386-89 (1970); G. C. Cook, Metabolism 17: 1073-83 (1968); and G. C. Cook, Nature 215: 1295-96 (1976).

7.

1. T. M. S. Wolever, Metabolism 39: 947-51 (1990).

2. J. A. Jenkins et al., Am. J. Clin. Nutr. 42: 604-17 (1985).

3. B. A. Swinburn et al., J. Clin. Endocrinol. Metab. 73: 156-65 (1991).

4. A. Walter et al., *Exerpta Medica:* 434-44 (1981).
5. W. E. Connor and S. L. Connor, *Med. Clin. N, AM* 66: 485-518 (1982).
6. T. M. S. Wolever et al., *Diabetic Medicine* 9: 451-58 (1992).
7. A. M. Fontvielle et al., *Diabetic Medicine* 9: 444-50 (1992).
8. B. A. Swinburn et al., *J. Clin. Endocrinol. Metab.* 73: 156-65 (1991).
9. J. E. Bundell, *Int. J. Obesity* 11: (suppl. 1): 9-25 (1987).
10. J. C. Brand et al., *Appetitet* 18: 129-41 (1992).
11. P. Leathwood and P. Pollet, *Appetite* 10: 1-10 (1988).
12. J. Stevens et al., *Am. J. Clin. Nutr.* 46: 812-17 (1987).
13. A. S. Levine et al., *Am. J. Clin. Nutr.* 50: 1303-7 (1989).
14. G. M. Ward et al., *Eur. J. Clin. Invest.* 12: 93-96 (1982); D. Porte and S. C. Woods, *Diabetologia* 20: 274-80 (1981); I. J. Stein et al., *Endocrinol.* 113: 299-301 (1983); J. Rodin et al., *Metabolism* 34: 826-31 (1985); S. J. Bhathena et al., *Proc. Soc. Exp. Biol. Med.* 181: 71-77 (1986); R. Schmid et al., *J. Clin. Endocrinol. Metabol.* 68: 1106 (1989); Y. B. Lombardo et al., *Horm. Metab. Res.* 25: 69-76 (1983); and N. Geary, *Neuroscience Behav. Rev.* 14: 323-338 (1990).
15. K. J. Acheson et al., *Am. J. Clin. Nutr.* 45: 78-85 (1987); Y.-J. Hannele et al., *Diabetes* 39: 157-67 (1990); G. D. Foster et al., *Am. J. Clin. Nutr.* 51: 167-72 (1990); and T. A. Wadden et al., *JAMA* 264: 707-11 (1980).
16. R. A. Mathieson et al., *Metabolism* 35: 394-99 (1986); and S. W. Spaulding et al., *J. Clin. Endocrinol. Metabol.* 46: 197-200 (1976).
17. M. F. Saad et al., *New Eng. J. Med.* 319:1500-06 (1988).

18. J. C. Brand et al., *Am. J. Clin. Nutr.* 51: 416-20 (1990).
19. Knowler et al., *Am. J. Clin. Nutr.* 53: 1543S-51S (1991).
20. A. W. Thornburn et al., *Am. J. Clin. Nutr.* 46: 282-85 (1987).
21. Ibid.
22. B. A. Swinburn et al., *J. Clin. Endocrinol. Metab.* 73: 156-65 (1991).
23. J. C. Brand et al., *Diabetes Care* 14: 95-101 (1991).
24. D. J. A. Jenkins et al., *Am. J. Clin. Nutr.* 48: 248-54 (1988); and A. M. Fontevielle et al., *Diabetes Nutr. Metab.* 1: 139-44 (1988).
25. J. C. Brand et al., *Diabetes Care* 14: 95-101 (1991).
26. R. K. Bernstein, *Diabetes, Type II.* Englewood Cliffs, NJ: Prentice Hall (1990).
27. F. Grande et al., *J. Nutr.* 86: 313-17 (1965).
28. J. W. Anderson et al., *Am. J. Clin. Nutr.* 51: 1013-19 (1990).
29. R. Doll and R. Peto, *J. Nat. Cancer. Inst.* 66: 1191-1308 (1981); and Washington, DC: National Cancer Institute, *Cancer Rates and Risks.* (1985).
30. S. Graham et al., *J. Nat. Cancer Inst.* 70: 687-92 (1983); and National Research Council *Diet, Nutrition and Cancer,* Washington DC: National Academy Press (1982).
31. A. S. Turstwell, *Eur. J. Clin. Nutr.* 46: (Suppl. 2); S91-S101 (1992).
32. D. E. Thomas et al., *Int. J. Sports Med.* 12: 180-86 (1991).

Appendix 1.

1. Quoted in H. Trowell, *Plant Foods for Man* 1: 157-68 (1975).

Index